HAUSWALDTS SPORT-STANGEN
CHOCOLADE.

Schwerter-
Chocolade Cacao

Riedel & Engelmann
Dresden

KAKAO
DEUTSCHMEISTER
mit Silberprämien

Petzold & Aulhorn A:G. Dresden-A.

Schwerter-
Cacao Chocolade
Riedel & Engelmann
Dresden

CHOCOLAT

GRAND PRIX   PARIS 1900

SUCHARD

Spezialität: Cacao-Pulver

Moser-Roth
STUTTGART.

Velma

CHOCOLAT SUCHARD
AROMATISCH u. FEINSCHMELZEND

Sarotti BERLIN

N=Nuss-Schokolade

DRE

Schutzmarke

Chocoladen & Zuckerwarenfabrik
DRESDEN

Kakao
Deutschmeister
mit Silberprämien

Petzold & Aulhorn A:G. Dresden-A.

CACAO

SUCHARD

Schokolade gibt Kraft.

WEZEL & NAUMANN A-G LEIPZIG-R.

CHOCOLATE
THE SWEET HISTORY

BETH KIMMERLE

PORTLAND, OREGON

Designer: Mary Ruhl
Cover Photo: Joe Felzman Photography
Project Manager: Jennifer Weaver-Neist
Editor: Ann Granning Bennett

Library of Congress Cataloging-in-Publication Data

Kimmerle, Beth, 1969-

Chocolate : the sweet history / Beth Kimmerle.-- 1st American ed.

p.   cm.

Includes bibliographical references.

ISBN 1-933112-04-2 (hardcover : alk. paper)

1. Chocolate--History.   2. Cookery (Chocolate) I. Title.

TX767.C5K56 2005

641.3'374--dc22

2004025961

Printed in Singapore

9 8 7 6 5 4 3 2 1

Collectors Press books are available at special discounts for bulk purchases, premiums, and promotions. Special editions, including personalized inserts or covers, and corporate logos, can be printed in quantity for special purposes. For further information contact: Special Sales, Collectors Press, Inc., P.O. Box 230986, Portland, OR 97281. Toll free: 1-800-423-1848.

For a free catalog write:
Collectors Press, Inc.
P.O. Box 230986
Portland, OR 97281
Toll free: 1-800-423-1848
collectorspress.com

Contents

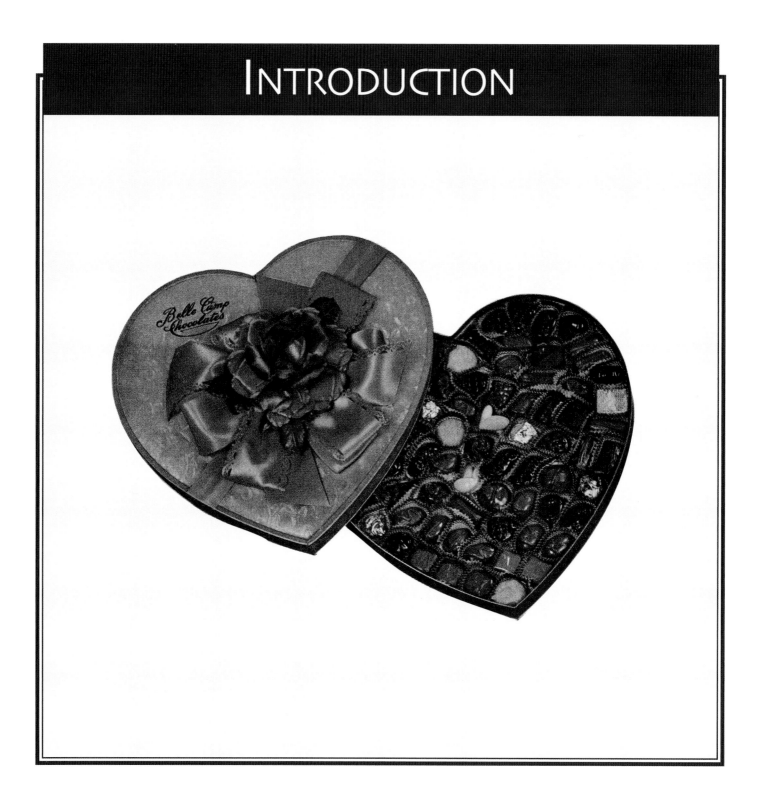

While researching my book, *Candy: The Sweet History*, I confirmed my long-held suspicion. There is a huge difference between candy and chocolate. They are two different worlds, intertwined yet quite separate. Their difference lies in their composition. Chocolate can stand alone, while candy is comprised of various elements. Chocolate starts with roasted cacao nibs, the amazingly elaborate and intense little seeds harvested from cacao pods, while candy usually begins as a simple cooked sugar base.

Chocolate is an exceptional food and ingredient because of the cacao plant's many varieties. The plants thrive in tropical regions that are all equidistant from the equator, but they produce vastly different pods. Varieties include trinitario, criollo, and forastero, and each has unique characteristics. Plantations employ drying methods to account for the broad array of distinct-tasting fermented beans. In fact, combining cacao beans to produce a chocolate recipe is much like blending grapes for wine.

Cacao can become a solid, a liquid, or a powder; the ways in which it can be transformed are almost limitless. Chocolate comprises several hundred complex chemicals, including stimulants and antioxidants that are now understood to have a positive effect on heart and health. Simply put, chocolate is an intricate food hailing from a natural source that has captivated and enthralled consumers for ages. It is in a league of its own.

When it is dark and smooth-melting with well-balanced flavors, I find chocolate irresistible. And I am not alone in my chocolate appreciation. Chocolate is the top-ranking flavor for most Americans. It has a wonderful taste and its miracle chemicals can both stimulate and calm our senses. Associated with indulgence, decadence, celebrations, and romance, it is really the only food I can think of that has such a dedicated following. The term chocoholic is a little silly, but many people are very habitual eaters — and most proudly so.

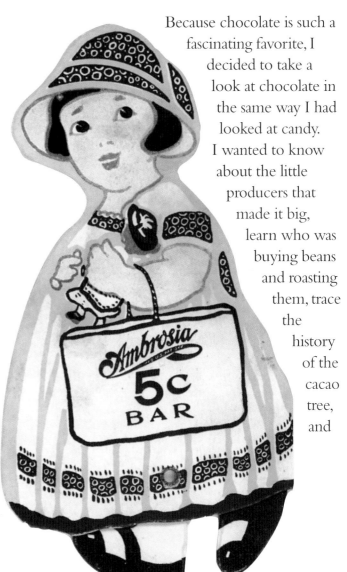

Because chocolate is such a fascinating favorite, I decided to take a look at chocolate in the same way I had looked at candy. I wanted to know about the little producers that made it big, learn who was buying beans and roasting them, trace the history of the cacao tree, and

1918 promotional advertising card with spinning feet for Milwaukee's Ambrosia Chocolates.
Courtesy Michael Rosenberg Collection

discover which companies have contributed to how we manufacture and consume chocolate today. This project is an exploration from bean to bar of the delicious foodstuff we call chocolate.

I went into this project with industry knowledge coupled with some understanding of processing and tasting. I soon discovered, however, that becoming a true expert takes many years of study and research and requires ongoing schooling. Determined to take a serious step into the chocolate vat, I immersed myself in visiting factories, both tasting and making chocolate. Simultaneously, I studied those companies that have had an impact on the American chocolate industry.

My true chocolate history began well before I entered into the confection industry; it started when I was very young. I was never deterred by the unsweetened baking squares I sampled from our kitchen cupboards. I always went back for more, convinced that somehow they would transform themselves into the sweet creamy flavor that chocolate really was to me. When a homemade cake or brownie was made from the parchment wrapped bitter blocks, I would believe again that baking chocolate must be sweet and that I had been wrong. I would go back to the cabinet and taste another pungent sample. At an early age I became a tenacious tester.

One of my early favorites was Frango Mints. They were developed in Seattle and sold in Frederick & Nelson Company department stores. In 1929, Chicago-based department store Marshall Field's acquired Frederick and Nelson and Franco Mints. Franco came from the "Fr" in Frederick; the "a" in and; the "n" in Nelson; and the "co" in company. But in the mid-1930s, when the Spanish Civil War broke out and Generalissimo Francisco Franco came into power, the mints were changed to Frango.

I was in junior high the first time I saw Marshall Field's Frango Mints produced.

I was captivated by the small brown squares gracefully marching down a belt to be bathed in a chocolate waterfall. The concept that candy was really and truly made by people in a working factory was riveting. It was like that classic chocolate factory episode of *I Love Lucy* coming to life! The little bright-green, half-pound, rectangle Frango box that I eyed at Marshall Field's seemed more special once I knew how its rich contents were made. That first factory visit created a mighty minty, extra velvety, and somehow more delicious Frango experience.

To this day, receiving an invitation to tour a factory is a very exciting moment for me. Viewing production is simply thrilling, like a violinist getting a peek into the seventeenth-century workshop of Stradivarius or a painter visiting a museum that houses the work that inspires his own.

When recalling my chocolate childhood, I must note the hundreds, perhaps thousands, of bars of World's Finest Chocolate I sold to support our various Y.M.C.A. ski trips and club events. In the early 1980s, as both a hungry and diligent entrepreneur, I combed the streets of my neighborhood, smiling at the friendly local folk, most of whom did not require the full sales pitch. They eyed the white, corrugated, World's Finest fundraising case and peeled off a bill in exchange for what was, at the time, a mammoth milk chocolate bar. I once made a total score while visiting a kind neighbor, who in retrospect was perhaps diabetic. She let me keep the money and also insisted I keep the very candy bar I was attempting to sell. The savvy youthful entrepreneur in me attempted to sell the bonus bar and make a little extra cash to deposit in my savings account. But inevitably, the chocolate carrier case became too heavy, despite the bustling sales from that evening; the air became a little cold; and the faint smell of fresh milk chocolate crept into the night. I ended up peeling away the slick white-with-gold embossed World's Finest Chocolate wrapper and looked under the gold foil to take just one bite.

I recently tasted a World's Finest Chocolate bar and, to my surprise, it tasted precisely the same as it did

The Chocolate Cigarettes contained in this package are manufactured within the meaning of the Federal Food, Drug & Cosmetic Act of 1939.

that night. I found that the manufacturer follows the same recipe used over fifty years ago in concocting its chocolate. In addition, the firm is one of only ten U.S. companies that produce chocolate straight from the bean.

As a special treat, my father occasionally brought home small white paper bags of white speckled, dark chocolate nonpariels from the local Fannie May store. It was conveniently located on the ground floor of his North Michigan Avenue office building. One time my small, greedy hands opened the bag and I found a shriveled insect antenna that wasn't fully covered in chocolate. My nose wrinkled, and I am sure I looked at my dad in horror.

I was told it was a chocolate-covered orange peel. This new discovery was both unexpected and perplexing to a child who associated citrus peel with the bitterness of the white pith that protects the juicy flesh of fruit. They quickly reminded me that the chocolate-candied peels were my grandmother's favorite. She has pretty decent taste, my little head thought. I probably remembered her homemade chocolate brownies and her well-stocked candy collection stashed away in a vintage Schrafft's tin. I first tried to slip the dark chocolate away from the slimy peel but it wouldn't budge. I finally decided to try the crazy concoction. Highly skeptical until the last moment, I tasted something that day that would forever stay with me. It would make me a fan of slathering copious amounts of orange marmalade on a warm chocolate croissant. The taste was slightly bitter and tart and was complimented perfectly with

the ideal amount of dark chocolate. Today, I remain a devotée to the classic and underappreciated dark-chocolate-covered orange peel.

Later, I developed confection products for Archibald Candy, the now defunct parent company that ran Fannie May and Fanny Farmer Candies. I had the dream job of working with research and development. I tasted, tested, and decided on new candies for hundreds of stores. Archibald Candy was a candy maker but did not process chocolate. Instead, an 18-wheel tanker truck delivered it. It arrived a few times a week, depending on the season, and was greeted by a taster who was responsible for insuring the delivery was of quality chocolate.

As tasting is largely about smelling, this special task was performed by sipping and smelling a large Pyrex beaker of liquid chocolate. A tanker carrying 44 tons of the sweet liquid rolled in and a pipeline tunneled the chocolate into the factory to become part of a vast array of classic buttercreams, Pixies, and Trinidads. After the taste test was completed and the tanker was emptied, another employee donned a white Tyvek suit and descended into the hole at the top of the tanker to squeegee out the remaining liquid. (I looked forward to the arrival of the tanker truck immensely and enjoyed the concept of a circular chocolate cavern on wheels.)

Blommer's, a Chicago company, supplied the Archibald factory with tons of chocolate. The River West factory was built in 1939, at the end of the Depression. I knew of Blommer's before I entered

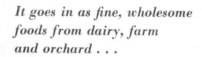

NOTE: If you candy is scarce the member sugar is rationed. Candy doing their best— can't find your fav other fine candies.

It goes in as fine, wholesome foods from dairy, farm and orchard . . .

It comes out

Candy

Candy at Christmas,
Candy all year;
Candy's nutritious
As well as good cheer.

Luscious fruits . . . pure milk . . . g
butter . . . fresh eggs . . . snowy sug
meaty nuts . . . tempting chocolate .
these and more. Each adds a part t
body's nutrition as it beckons the ap
with flavor.

Of course, you know that candy—
box or bagful—is a splendid sour
quick energy. But take a *modern* lo
candy, and the things candy is made
and you'll really realize why it's
human to reach for candy.

Council on Candy of the
National Confectioners'
Association

Headquarters: One North
LaSalle Street,
Chicago 2, Illinois

Candy is a Delicious Food

. . . an organization devoted to maintaining high standards of quality in candy and the dissemination of authoritative information on its use as an energy-producing, morale-building food.

into the world of confections. I discovered it by accident one afternoon. I worked several blocks from the factory and had parked my car close to where the cacao beans were roasted and turned into chocolate. After long hours at my job in the Chicago Merchandise Mart, I arrived at my vehicle and felt surrounded by a cloud of delightful goodness. The sweet aroma permeated the night air surrounding the factory, and I parked my car on the street intentionally just to have a post-work waft of the heavenly substance. Blommer's is still family-owned and operated and is one of the few factories producing finished chocolate from cocoa beans.

After many years of being around and investigating chocolate, I have incredible memories and a clear taste for exactly what I like, not to mention an adventurous spirit to sample almost anything made with the chocolate substance. My personal chocolate journey has been fantastic and educational, but

nothing compares to the journey of this amazing little bean. This aptly named "Food of the Gods," started as the main ingredient of a frothy drink in the Americas, moved to Europe to get sweetened, evolved further from its pure beginnings, and returned to the Americas to bask in the kitchens of pastry chefs and the mouths of connoisseurs.

With this book, I honor and explore the heritage of this sweet substance, reveal where it's been, and predict where it is headed. It is a look into our collective, cherished, chocolate past and a peek into the possibilities of a perfect chocolate future.

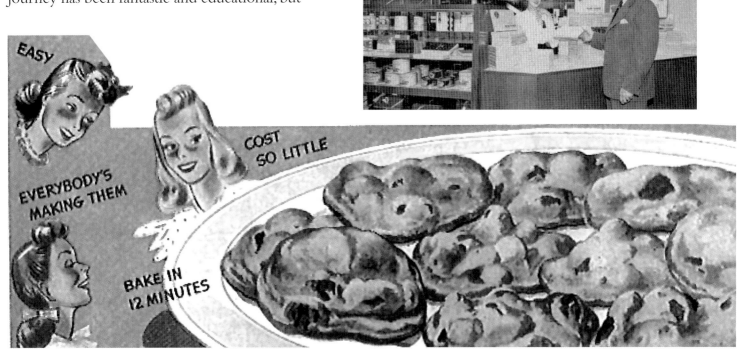

THE HISTORY OF CHOCOLATE

CHAPTER ONE

Truffles, doughnuts, cacao beans, nonpareils, chocolate chips, chocolate-covered nuts, cakes, baking chocolate, cacao nibs, pastilles, chocolate bars, ice cream, syrup, and mocha coffee and milk. Chocolate is everywhere. We usually think of chocolate as the sweet, usually solid substance of present times. But our universal love affair with chocolate began thousands of years ago when it was a consumed mainly as a beverage. The history of chocolate and how it progressed from a Mesoamerican drink into a globally coveted flavor and food spans many cultures and continents. Chocolate has lived in our instincts, hearts, and senses for thousands of years. A simple chocolate bar may seem straight-forward. It is a veritable treasure chest, however, holding many memories that have been handed down from generation to generation.

Chocolate history begins with its source, the tropical cacao tree. And all chocolate products start with the cacao

tree that originated in the upper Amazon Basin. It was identified as a crucial crop more than 2,000 years ago when it grew in the tropical rainforests of Mesoamerica. The dirigible-shaped fruit of the cacao tree contains seeds that are processed into chocolate. The first people known to have produced chocolate from the cacao plant were the ancient cultures of what is now Mexico and Central America. These

people mixed ground and roasted cacao seeds with water, chili peppers, and cornmeal, producing a paste that, when mixed with water, made a frothy, bitter, and spicy chocolate drink.

For the Olmec peoples of the Gulf Coast of Mexico, chocolate was likely cultivated and became a part of religious and social lives. The Olmec culture flourished from around 1200 to 300 B.C.; they were the first Mesoamerican people to develop the concept of zero, utilize a calendar, build and sculpt striking structures, and create a writing system. These early achievements, along with Olmec myths and rituals, would later become the strengths of Maya and Aztec societies. The earliest evidence of chocolate use dates to around 600 B.C. Residue of cocoa has been discovered in jugs that were used to pour and store a liquid chocolate drink. The spicy cocoa paste and water were poured back and forth between jugs to produce a lathered beverage.

But it was when the ancient Maya cultivated cacao between 250-900 A.D. that its use began to spread to nearby regions where it grew indigenously. The Maya lived on the Yucatan Peninsula, in what is now Southern Mexico, where wild cocoa trees grew. They cultivated the tree, originally found in nearby lush rainforests close to their villages, creating the first cocoa farms. They harvested the fruit and later roasted the beans that would be ground into a paste to form a drink they called "xocoatl."

The word chocolate is said to derive from this Mayan term "xocoatl" and cocoa from the Aztec name "cacahuatl." The native Mayan term "xoco" means foam and "atl" means water, as early chocolate was consumed in liquid form and a large crest of foam topping the drink was valued. It has been noted that derivations of the term for chocolate and cocoa show up in many Mesoamerican words for a number of places and things, ranging from everyday implements to towns. This implies that chocolate had an iconic significance, and its importance to the culture was deep-rooted.

The Maya were well-known chocoholics, and many vessels have been found that depict their fondness for the fluid. These are the practical wares in which they served chocolate and also the ceremonial vessels used in celebrations and services. In addition to being fine

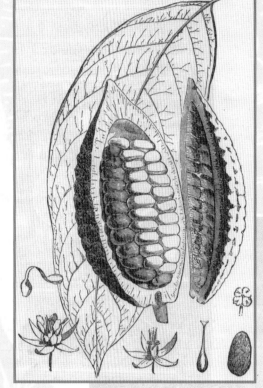

cultivators, the Maya were great writers and illustrators; they left behind colorful manuscripts explaining their intricate relationship with chocolate. In their texts, they vividly recount cacao preparation, recipes, and ceremonial significance, as well as descriptions about the monetary value of cacao.

As cacao grew into a full-scale commodity, the prized cocoa beans were used as currency for valuable gifts and in trading. Merchants and farmers traded cacao beans and other goods with neighboring Aztecs and thereby spread the popularity of cocoa use around the region. Most Maya could occasionally drink chocolate but, because of its value, the Mayan royalty particularly favored it.

Images courtesy New York Public Library

By the fourteenth century the Aztecs had created a powerful, dominant empire and controlled a sizable segment of central Mexico. These ancient Aztecs founded the great city of Tenochtitlán around 1325. It became the greatest metropolis in the area later named Central Mexico. It was prosperous and powerful, full of culture, and rich in Mexican tradition. Tenochtitlán was a vast complex made up of smaller cities and waterways; it was the epicenter of Mesoamerican civilization.

The valley of Central Mexico had a dry climate, and the Aztecs were unable to grow the valued cocoa trees that needed a fertile, lush environment in order to survive. Therefore, they obtained a steady supply of cocoa beans by way of "tribute" or trade. Tribute was a feudal system of taxation paid by districts conquered by the domineering Aztecs. The well-trained Aztec armies were matchless and able to quickly assume governance of surrounding cities. The cocoa drink became an army elixir. Served in a ceremonial cup made from a hollow gourd or decorated pottery, it was a refreshing and nourishing drink that warriors consumed before battle.

The Aztecs established consistent trade interaction with the subservient Maya and adopted their beverage-making methods and drinking customs. The Aztec served their spicy drink like the Maya and may have introduced new flavors like vanilla and wild-bee honey to the drink. The Aztec brew was still pungent for our tastes but, with the addition of honey and vanilla, it began to taste somewhat sweeter than the original basic brew. Sugarcane was not

This 1928 image shows workers splitting pods to gather seeds from the cacao fruit. The seeds, or beans, were then spread in trays to dry in the tropical sun.
Courtesy New York Public Library

available to the ancient Mesoamericans; it was not locally grown and had not yet been introduced to the region.

The core of Aztec high society, the rulers, priests, and soldiers partook of the sacred blend. Priests offered cacao seeds to the gods; they served chocolate drinks during sacred ceremonies. The ancient Aztecs saw the cacao tree as a magical supplier of wealth and health and assigned their god Quetzalcoatl to be its protector.

The Aztecs had many gods, but it was Quetzalcoatl, god of civilization and learning, who is associated

with cacao beans. Great temples were built to honor him, and Montezuma, Emperor of Mexico and ruler of the Aztecs, revered him. An ancient myth explains that Quetzalcoatl was banished from earth for the blasphemous act of giving this sacred drink to humans. His devoted worshippers, who awaited his return, always remembered him.

Meanwhile his leafy legacy, the magical cocoa tree, remained abundant for his loving followers. When Hernán Cortés, the Spanish conquistador, arrived in 1519 with his fleet of galleons, it is rumored that the Aztecs thought he was Quetzalcoatl returning from a far-off paradise.

However, Hernán Cortés was in the region only to exploit the Aztec land and treasures and, while we can't know how he felt about being mistaken for a god, we do know he acted like a selfish one. The great city of Tenochtitlan was boldly destroyed by the Spanish conquerors and renamed Mexico City. By 1521, the Aztec empire had completely collapsed, the ruler Montezuma was defeated, and Spanish conquistadors controlled Mexico.

Years earlier, in 1502, Spanish explorer Christopher Columbus had captured a Mayan trading canoe near the island of Guanaja. The Mayan cargo included grains, metal wares, and fibers. He also noted that there were large seeds, resembling almonds, that seemed to have great value to the natives. But it was his fellow conquistador successor who later realized the value of the cacao bean.

In fact, eager to take advantage of its value, Cortés had meticulously documented the Aztec use of chocolate, even noting the fifty cups Montezuma consumed per day. He was intrigued with the concept of cacao having monetary value and soon established plantations in the name of the Spanish crown in order to cultivate cacao currency.

Back in Europe, a soft rendering of "xocolatl" was introduced to the Spanish court of King Charles V in 1520. The Spaniards changed the way the chocolate drink was prepared and flavored. A new beverage, enriched with sweeter and milder European flavorings, emerged. The Mesoamerican traditional tastes were too bitter and spicy for the European palate. Soon drink preparations were also distinguished, and instead of frothing between goblets, the Spanish concocted a *molinillo* or wooden whisk to fluff the beverage. This new Euro-agreeable chocolate beverage was a favorite of the Spanish king and his royal court.

The drink seeped through Spain and quickly became popular, although it remained a limited, luxurious drink made only on a small scale. But by 1585, the first official large shipments of cocoa beans arrived at the port of Seville from Mexico. Cocoa grew in the overseas colonies of Peru, Jamaica, and Venezuela and ended Spain and Portugal's exclusive hold on the delicacy.

While sipping the popular drink, anecdotes of the beverage's origins filled grand rooms around the palaces of Spain. People spoke of the ancient beverage's qualities, eliciting conversations about secret somas, warrior elixirs, and healing medicines. Eager to understand the powers of their favorite new beverage, Spaniards wanted to classify the new drink according to the popular medical theory based on the humoral system. Cacao escaped easy identification and, while health qualities of chocolate were deliberated, it grew immensely in popularity. As physicians debated its properties, rumors of its aphrodisiac qualities started to surface. As only aristocracy enjoyed it, legends about its exclusivity escalated.

Religious leaders also questioned chocolate. They were concerned with whether it was a beverage or a food, since strict, church-ordered fasts forbade consuming any nourishment from night until morning. It was finally agreed that as a drink, it did not officially break the fast. This may have been because many friars and priests who worked in the New World had grown attached to the popular beverage. Perhaps the Spanish monks, those who safely guarded the recipes for making chocolate, wanted to see it pass into suitable standing. Whatever the reasons, the good news that the beverage was both nutritious and accepted by the Church elevated its status even further.

As it is always difficult to keep something so fine hidden from others, Spain's close neighbors were introduced to drinking chocolate soon after. By the early 1600s, the clandestine chocolate drink traveled to Italy, France, and England. The arrival of chocolate coincided with the appearance of other hot beverages, coffee from the Middle East and tea from China. But only chocolate would continue to maintain such a delicate combination of traits: exclusive, romantic, sinfully indulgent, seductive, exotic, delicious, and yet healthful and nutritious.

In 1615, the French became aware of cocoa, almost a century after the discovery of the chocolate drink by the Spanish court. Spanish princess Anne of Austria married French King Louis XIII and introduced the drinking of chocolate to the French court. Later, chocolate was hugely popular in the court of Louis

Spanish friars and monks took to drinking the New World drink as it was considered healthy and did not break obligatory fasts.
Courtesy New York Public Library

The Chocolate Shop Postcard, dated 1950, advertises, "A wide variety of home-made candies. A real taste thrill in every piece!" Courtesy Beth Kimmerle Collection

Phillips Digestible Cocoa calendar postcard, mid-1800s.
Courtesy
Beth Kimmerle Collection

Rose Package

LAKESIDE CHOCOLATES

Beautiful postcards advertised chocolate and were easy to slip into fancy chocolate boxes as reminders of where to buy the next pound. (Above) Lakeside Chocolates half-pound box; Chicago, 1915.
Courtesy Michael Rosenberg Collection

XIV. The Sun King's first wife, Maria Teresa, who grew up in Spain, likely enjoyed it. Madame du Barry, the insatiable mistress of Louis XV of France, was reputed to encourage her lovers to drink chocolate in order to keep up with her. In France, as in most of Europe, chocolate enjoyed a fancy and frolicking reputation that continued to flourish for hundreds of years.

In fact, an enterprising Frenchman opened the first chocolate house in London in 1657. The shop was called The Coffee Mill and Tobacco Roll, and it served beverages and other highly stylish items from the New World, including chocolate. Costing a whopping ten to fifteen shillings per pound, chocolate was considered a pricey beverage for the elite businessmen of the day. However, with the addition of chocolate to menus, chocolate became available to those who were not royalty and nobility. It remained expensive, mostly due to taxes imposed, long after tea and coffee were affordable to the middle classes.

By the early 1700s, it was Italy's chocolatiers who became known throughout Europe as true artists of New World ingredients like chocolate and sugar. Gianduja, a chocolate hazelnut paste named for the small island where Columbus first saw cacao beans, became a popular nut-enhanced chocolate variation. New World plantations, owned by Spain and later the Dutch, began to turn out vast quantities of cacao, and chocolate developed into an affordable and widely available ingredient. Other flavors, both exotic and common, were combined with chocolate during the initial experimentation years. With prices dropping, chocolate began to appear in cakes and confections served in cafés, pastry shops, and delicacy emporiums. Compressed chocolate cakes began to be sold at apothecaries and food shops. The widespread availability slowly pushed chocolate from solely a drink with medicinal value to a flavoring and later an eating bar.

By the mid-eighteenth century, chocolate secured a place on the list of items that became fully integrated into European and colonial life. Cacao was assigned its botanical title *Theobroma cacao*, meaning "food of the gods," while the New World collided with the Old. The Industrial Revolution and American Revolution further steered chocolate production, preference, and acceptance.

In 1773, when furious American colonists were fed up with taxation on tea, their hot beverage of choice, they dumped incoming cargo into Boston's Charles River. They began to import cacao from nearby producing colonies in the Caribbean Islands, thereby circumventing England's taxes. Chocolate soon became a colonial favorite for making a hot beverage. Colonists enjoyed its theoretical medicinal purposes and the symbolic statement it made against the growing strife with England.

Early American chocolate makers sold chocolate by grinding beans on a metate, a traditional grinding implement, and forming it into cakes. Quakers accepted chocolate for its health and medicinal values and believed drinking chocolate was much healthier than alcohol. Many Quakers settled in the

Philadelphia area, and English chocolate manufacturers Joseph Rowntree and George Cadbury later based their chocolate-making business models on their Quaker religious principles. (Hershey's Mennonite background steered his successful business.) New York City, formerly Dutch-owned New Amsterdam, was influenced by strong trading ties with its previous owner. The Dutch controlled many colonies that grew cacao beans, and colonial New York benefited, while hosting a booming chocolate industry.

Using direct imports, early American chocolate makers and physicians explored the possibilities of commerce and chocolate. In 1765, Dr. James Baker, an apothecary proprietor from Massachusetts, and Irishman John Hannon collectively formed a chocolate-manufacturing enterprise. Using a local

gristmill, they ground cacao beans into chocolate paste and molded it into cakes for drinking chocolate. Their company was originally called Hannon's Best Chocolate. John Hannon was later thought to be lost at sea while on a cacao-buying trip to the West Indies. The company was renamed the Baker Company and remained in the Baker family until it was bought by General Foods in 1927. Baker's Chocolate still produces a line of baking chocolate and is currently owned by Kraft Foods. Baker's Chocolate touts the oldest grocery product trademark in the United States today.

Meanwhile, a doctor across the pond was mechanizing his chocolate-making operation. Joseph Fry, an English physician and Quaker, was a strong believer in the health qualities of cocoa. His sons purchased a Watts steam engine for grinding cacao beans for their family chocolate-making business. This evolution led to the manufacture of chocolate on a massive scale and made Fry chocolates available to a wide audience. When Joseph Fry died in 1787, his chocolate business was taken over by his three grandsons: Joseph, Francis, and Richard. Under their management, the company continued to expand. Later, in 1847, while the company was in the hands of Joseph Fry's great-grandson, the company mixed sugar and cocoa butter back into defatted, cocoa powder to create a substance that could successfully be molded into edible bars. The resulting chocolate block was an innovation, albeit still rather bitter. Due to Fry's creation, eating chocolate would soon be as popular as consuming it as a beverage. Because of their discovery, Fry became the biggest European chocolate maker and the first to produce chocolate bars at a significant level. In 1919, J. S. Fry & Sons merged with Cadbury Brothers.

Fry's chocolate bar advancements were made possible by the availability of defatted cocoa powder. It was Coenraad van Houten, a chemist and chocolate manufacturer from Amsterdam, who perfected the extraction of the natural cocoa butter from cocoa beans. With his patented technology, crushed beans were pressed separating chocolate liquor from the fatty cocoa butter. His invention further pushed chocolate from a beverage to a confection and improved the quality of chocolate by giving it a

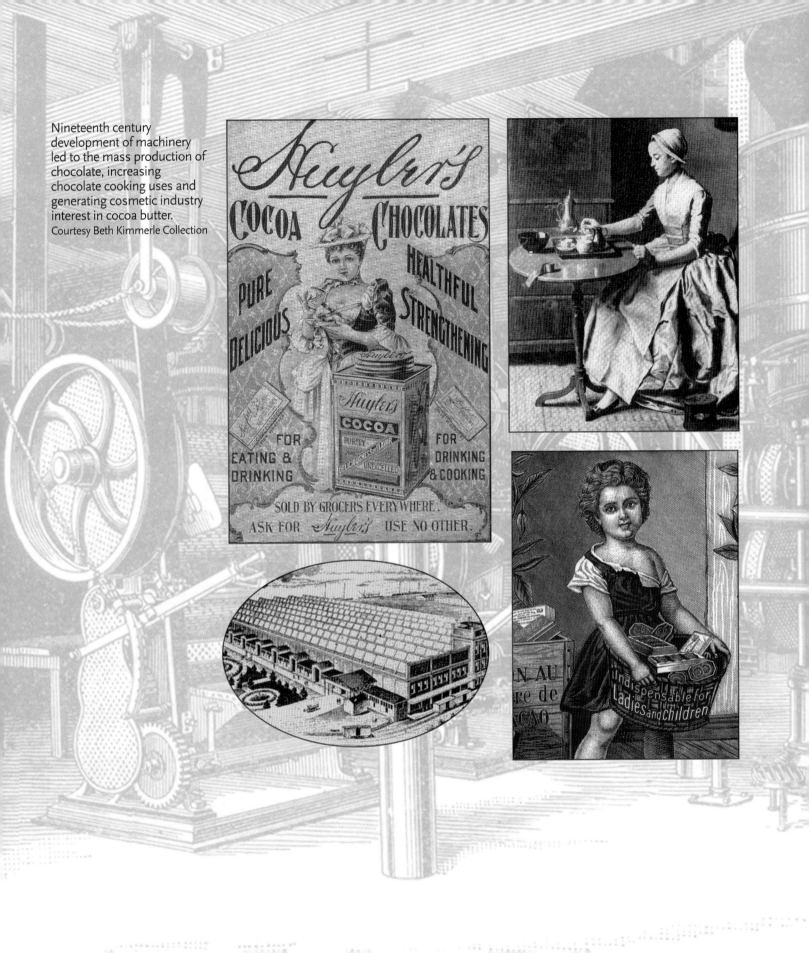

Nineteenth century development of machinery led to the mass production of chocolate, increasing chocolate cooking uses and generating cosmetic industry interest in cocoa butter.
Courtesy Beth Kimmerle Collection

smoother consistency. To make his defatted fine particles easier to mix with water, he developed an alkaline treatment, which made the powder darker and also alleviated some of the bitterness. Van Houten's alkalizing process became known as "dutching" and alkalized cocoa is still popular today.

In 1824, John Cadbury, a Quaker from Birmingham, England, opened a small grocery store. He began to experiment with grinding cocoa at his shop until chocolate became his best-selling item. John and his brother Benjamin formed a partnership to wholesale his successful chocolate, and later the business was transferred to John's sons, Richard and George. Cadbury's chocolate became a favorite in England at a time when chocolate tastes and production styles were regionalizing. The company received a Royal Warrant to act as the sole purveyor of cocoa and chocolates to Queen Victoria. She remained a loyal Cadbury customer, and in 1899, she sent half a million pounds of the chocolate to her troops stationed in South Africa during the Boer War. The chocolate was sent in generic, unbranded tins, as Cadbury's Quaker ethics made him conscientiously anti-war.

Throughout the final years of the nineteenth century, Cadbury dominated the British marketplace with fine cocoas and chocolates. It was also the first to package chocolates in fanciful boxes, and in 1868 the first to sell chocolates in a heart-shaped box to honor St. Valentine's Day. The Cadbury concept of a seasonal box led to new packaging improvements and advertising methods to further the advancement and distribution of chocolate around the world. In 1879, the company built a factory in Bournville, England, and provided housing and recreational facilities to employees; it was a model that later inspired Milton Hershey.

The Cadbury family maintained their Quaker ideals, even as their business grew into a triumphant industry. Much of their profit, however, was based on slave-grown cocoa from Africa, and toward the beginning of the twentieth century, Cadbury struggled with improving working conditions on plantations. Unfortunately, the cacao industry and chocolate makers still strain today with the question of how to sell large quantities of chocolate, while treating workers and farmers fairly and paying them reasonable wages.

In mid-nineteenth century Switzerland, Rudolphe Lindt, Daniel Peter, and Henri Nestlé were innovating and experimenting in the blossoming business of chocolate. Lindt, in his quest to create a chocolate that was not as brittle and dry as others on the market, created a machine

The Dutch became established in chocolate, as many early Dutch colonies produced and grew cacao. In 1828, Dutchman Coenraad van Houten invented a press that extracted cocoa butter from cocoa solids. The process is still used today, and the resulting powder is referred to as "Dutched cocoa."
Courtesy Beth Kimmerle Collection

that subtly stirred the chocolate over a slab of marble with rollers. His apparatus was called a conching machine, as the rollers were seashell-shaped. His creamy concoctions were smoother and glossier than most and became known as fondant-style chocolate. His conching process became customary in chocolate making and is still used today. By 1899, Rudolphe Lindt sold the formula for making his creamy chocolate to David Sprüngli. Their combined chocolate venture became the well-known Swiss confection business Lindt & Sprüngli.

Fellow Swiss countryman, Daniel Peter, was on another pursuit. Peter experimented intently on infusing chocolate with milk. He was after a recipe that would mellow the bitterness of the cocoa bean but also cut the more expensive cacao with a filler ingredient. Peter was eager to model a solid bar similar in taste to that of the chocolate and milk drink preferred by many chocolate consumers.

Concurrently, Henri Nestlé was in the infant-food formula business and was working on making various milk recipes that would stay fresh. He developed a method for producing sweetened condensed milk, and this turned out to be the fulfillment of Daniel Peter's milk-chocolate dream. Nestlé's condensed milk was the magic touch

"MACK'S MILK CHOCOLATE."
THE BEST!
READY FOR INSTANT USE.
BOILING WATER ONLY REQUIRED.
IT IS PURE!

Mack's Trade cards and other chocolate ephemera have become highly collectible. This card from the late 1800s was supplied by H.H. Monson Grocers in New Haven, Connecticut.
Courtesy Beth Kimmerle Collection

needed for a creamy milk-chocolate bar that would not spoil. By 1879, Peter and Nestlé created a company that has evolved into the world's largest food and beverage company.

While chocolate became a booming international business, European chocolatiers began to migrate to the United States. Many brought with them confectionery skills that they aimed to explore in the land of plenty. French expatriates Louis Sherry and Henry Maillard set up elegant chocolate stores and cashed in on New York's opulent Gilded Age. During these years, industrialists accumulated great wealth and celebrated their riches as never before. Sherry's restaurants served dinners that were lavish and expensive, while Maillard's kitchens pumped out cakes and confections at a rapid rate. Both men enjoyed social and business success that made them very rich. They also introduced European methods to American chocolatiers, further globalizing chocolate production and recipes.

The promise of gold first motivated Etienne Guittard and Domingo Ghirardelli to travel to the West. But instead of becoming a forty-niner, the French Guittard started a business to supply San Francisco's newly affluent with chocolates. Today the founder's great-grandson Gary Guittard runs the family-

Cinderella stamps or Cinderellas, are sometimes rejected by serious collectors, as originally they had no value and were not valid as official, paid postage. Issued in the early 1900s, many Cinderella stamps were beautifully rendered, miniature versions of popular poster designs. Manufacturers inserted them into cans of cocoa and wrapped chocolate bars to promote their brands and commemorate products. They were also intended to entice consumers to purchase the product, thereby creating brand loyalty, and chocolate fans collected them in order to obtain awards and prizes offered by the issuers. Large chocolate companies like Nestlé issued poster-stamp albums to encourage poster-stamp collecting and saving.

owned Guittard. It is the largest privately owned chocolate company in the United States and one of ten companies that process raw cacao beans into chocolate. Italian-born confectioner Domingo Ghirardelli had witnessed the possibilities of the cacao business while in South America, and he started a chocolate factory after a brief shift in the Gold Rush. He began his business on monies saved by selling supplies to miners and was importing two hundred tons of beans annually to Northern California by 1885.

The World's Columbian Exposition in Chicago in 1893 had a huge impact on the American chocolate industry. The predecessor to the World's Fair concept, it was a platform for science and industry to show off their latest and greatest inventions. It was a phenomenally well-attended attraction for entrepreneurs and spectators alike; an exhibition named for the anniversary of Columbus landing in the New World. Chocolate was a well-represented category at the show; the United States alone was consuming 26 million pounds of chocolate per year. But international companies showed up, too, and Germany's Stollwerck Chocolate set up a majestic display comprised of thousands of pounds of intricately sculpted chocolate. Boston-based Lowney's Chocolate had an entire pavilion exhibiting hand-filled bon bons and primitive chocolate bars. A young fellow named Milton Hershey walked the halls in Chicago and witnessed a machinery demonstration that changed his thriving Pennsylvania caramel business into one that focused solely on chocolate.

Milton began the twentieth century by introducing Hershey's Milk Chocolate bar, and seven years later he was producing large quantities of a new little item called a Hershey's Kiss. His business grew so big that he soon was the unofficial emperor of a growing town named Hershey, Pennsylvania. He structured the town to include housing for workers, a rail system, a community center, a gymnasium, and much more. Hershey is one of the few early chocolate pioneers accountable for having introduced chocolate to the masses by producing a quality, consistent chocolate bar for an affordable price.

Otto J. Scholenleber started the Milwaukee-based Ambrosia Chocolate Company in 1894. It was named to honor chocolate's earlier divine usage. Ambrosia soon expanded into making chocolate bars for the first vending machines. Scholenleber's daughter Gretchen steered the company for many years. She became the president of Ambrosia Chocolate and in 1935 was named the first woman member of a commodity exchange, the New York Cocoa Exchange. Chocolate was breaking barriers; this prestigious position was unheard of for a woman at the time. In 1964, with the acquisition of Hooten Chocolate and W.R. Grace, Ambrosia's cocoa concentration shifted to

producing bulk-chocolate ingredients for the bakery, confectionery, dairy, and food service industries, servicing large companies such as Hostess, Pillsbury, and Nabisco. Food giant Archer Daniels Midland Company now owns Ambrosia and has become the world's premier processor of cacao beans.

As more American companies joined in the chocolate excitement, mass production and low material costs allowed almost everyone to enjoy a piece of chocolate on occasion. By the 1920s, chocolate was consumed widely as a solid eating bar, but hot cocoa was still very popular. Chocolate was viewed as nutritious and enriching and many companies marketed their products for children. Companies began to tout the health benefits of a five-cent chocolate bar as a cheap meal replacement to poor Depression-era consumers. Chocolate companies also began to mix other ingredients, like nuts, nougat, and caramel, with chocolate to create a candy-bar craze that seized America.

In 1923, Frank Mars, after years in the candy business, created the nougat-centered Milky Way candy bar; it was a huge sensation. In one year, sales increased from $72,800 to $792,000. By the early 1930s, Mars continued to experiment and developed instantly popular bars like Snickers and 3 Musketeers. In 1941, brightly colored pieces of candy-coated chocolate were formulated for United States military forces.

(Above) Sweet Milk Chocolate wrapper, circa 1918. Otto J. Scholenleber started Ambrosia Chocolate Company in 1894 and later produced chocolate for food companies such as Hostess, Pillsbury, and Nabisco. Courtesy Beth Kimmerle Collection

Image from 1926 Ghirardelli Chocolate educational charts, describing the chocolate growing and manufacturing process. This card shows the then revolutionary vacuum packing of ground chocolate. (Innovative packaging remains vital to preserving cocoa freshness and flavor.) Courtesy Beth Kimmerle Collection

They were a product of Forrest Mars, Frank's son, and Bruce Murrie, who worked for the Hershey Chocolate Company at the time. Their initials together formed the name "M&M." The letter M would soon be stamped on millions of brightly colored pellets. The candy with the slogan, "The milk chocolate melts in your mouth — not in your hand," is one of America's favorites.

By the 1970s, Mars's business expanded enormously, producing chocolate bars, pet products, drinks, and electronics. Today Mars is an international $14 billion company that shares the helm of the American chocolate marketplace with Hershey. Mars processes finished chocolate in nine plants dotting North America. They are a top buyer of raw cacao beans, as well as other derivatives like cocoa powder and cocoa butter.

The Draps family opened the original, elegant Godiva Chocolate shop on a Grande Place cobblestone street in Brussels, 1927. The same plaza also housed renowned chocolate praline company Neuhaus Chocolatier. The Campbell Soup Company purchased Godiva Chocolatier and introduced the concept of premium chocolate to America in 1966. Neuhaus was brought over a short time later and sold exclusively at the high-end retailer Neiman Marcus. Americans soon associated fine chocolates with intricately molded designs and beautifully elegant gold *ballotin*-box packaging. Belgium expats Godiva and Neuhaus started a shift towards premium, European-styled chocolate away from the standard, more modestly presented American favorites like Fanny Farmer, Schrafft's, and Loft's, a famous, now defunct East Coast candy store chain.

The last half of the twentieth century also saw an era of massive chocolate consolidation. In 1988 Nestlé bought the British chocolate manufacturer Rowntree, effectively making Nestlé the world's largest chocolate manufacturer. At the same time, Hershey's was on a brand-buying spree and bought Peter Paul, makers of Almond Joy and Mounds. Lindt and Sprüngli bought the classic American chocolate maker Ghirardelli. But while immense international chocolate companies were swallowing each another, some subtle trends started to emerge.

Recently, there has been an increasing movement towards fine, small production chocolates.

Consumers are recognizing boutique chocolate makers and are increasingly interested in those hand-making chocolate, using old-fashioned methods and quality ingredients. Chocolates infused with natural flavors and vivid spices are also popular. No longer satisfied with the basic, and perhaps bland, large-scale offerings, consumers want to experience organic, single-origin, and high cocoa content.

Another strong shift is back to American-made chocolates. Alice Medrich opened her Berkeley, California, store in 1977 and ushered in a boom of conscientious confectioners who wanted to make classic, delicious chocolates unadulterated by large-scale techniques. Others, too, were heading back to basics, and American chocolate companies like Lake Champlain, Joseph Schmidt, and Scharffen Berger emerged with the desire and business models to produce high-quality, well-crafted chocolates and confections. They've helped spawn a new generation of chocolatiers who are merging classic production processes with superior ingredients. No longer is it an axiom that choice chocolates must be imported from Belgium or Switzerland.

An added chocolate trend is the exploration of the positive health effects of chocolate. Throughout history, chocolate has been associated with medicinal benefits, but modern medicine is looking deeper to verify the facts. Chocolate has been officially cleared of the former allegations that it caused migraines, obesity, and acne. Recent research has shown that dark chocolate contains high levels of a kind of antioxidant called flavonoids. Scientists have identified that flavonoids raise blood pressure and heart rate by protecting blood vessels from the damaging effects of unstable oxygen compounds called free radicals. As cardiovascular disease is quickly becoming an epidemic, science is examining how chocolate, with its heart-protecting qualities, can become a bona fide healer.

Today, chocolate is America's top favorite flavor, and worldwide sales of the chocolate industry have topped $50 billion — no small beans by any measure. Chocolate has come a long way from a frothy Mesoamerican drink but is still worth its weight in gold. Controversy surrounds the rainforest-grown cacao crop and the labor that produces it. However, there are dedicated and competent companies and organizations making sure that social, environmental, and economical long-term solutions are formed and properly addressed.

Meanwhile, we continue to experiment with new uses and flavors, as well as gain further understanding about the true magic chocolate holds. With every moment we let a perfect piece melt on our tongues, the charmed history of chocolate continues.

Maillard's was an elite chocolate shop opened during New York's opulent Gilded Age. The shop remained a Manhattan luxury confectioner for years.
Courtesy New York Public Library

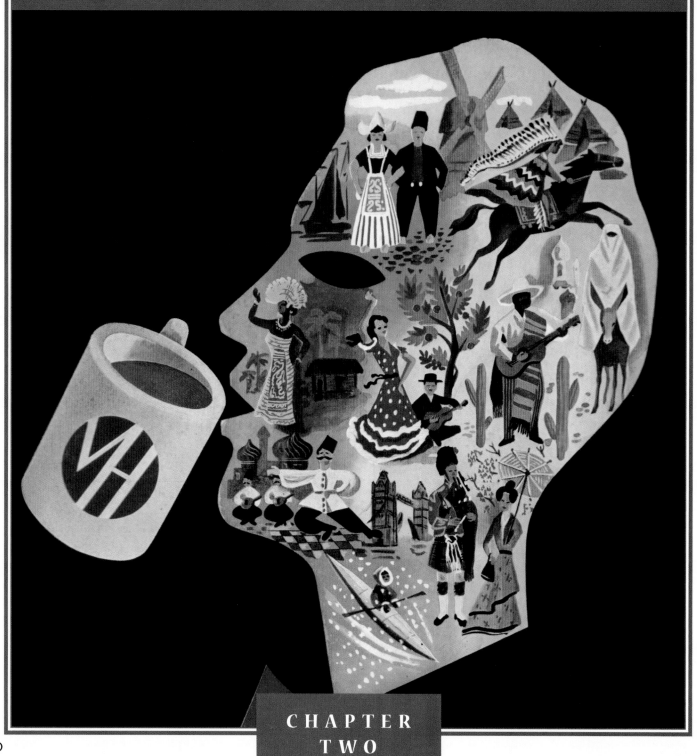

CHAPTER
TWO

1500~400 B.C

The Olmec Indian civilization is believed by many to be the first peoples to use and grow the cacao bean.

250~900 A.D.

Bringing the cacao tree out of the rainforest, the Maya establish cacao plantations throughout their kingdom, first in Guatemala and then upon immigrating to the Yucatan Peninsula. Primarily, roasted beans are ground and mixed with water and spices to create a cocktail for the social and military elite.

1000~1200

Throughout Mesoamerica, cacao continues to be used as the main ingredient for a paste, dissolved in water and taken as a beverage. The cocoa bean is used as both a unit of calculation and currency.

1200~1500

The Aztecs enjoy their chocolate in much the same way as the Maya, occasionally flavoring it with vanilla, allspice, chiles, and honey. The first to tax the bean, the Aztecs find their "xocalatl" (warm foamy liquid) an integral part of religious ceremony, a fortifying tonic for the warrior class, and a nourishing elixir for the privileged.

1502

Columbus becomes the first European to witness the uses of cacao during a voyage to what is now Nicaragua. However, the celebrated sailor misses the boat in regards to the bean's potential, doing little with his almond-like "souvenirs" upon his return to Europe.

1519

Hernán Cortés and his fellow Spaniards witness Montezuma drinking "xocalatl" and write that they've seen ". . . a drink that builds up resistance and fights fatigue."

1528

Inspired by the bean's use as currency, Cortés establishes a New World plantation in Spain's name, intent on proving that money can indeed grow on trees. The conquistador also returns to Europe with the beans and the means for making the chocolate drink. Many believe it was he who first sweetened the drink with sugar cane to make it palatable to Europeans tastes.

1585

The first commercially grown shipment of cacao arrives in Seville. The secret delicacy previously available only to Spain's elite soon spreads across Europe.

1615

Spanish princess Anne of Austria marries Louis XIII and shares her love of drinking chocolate with French royalty. She is said to have given her husband an engagement gift of chocolate packaged in an elegantly ornate chest. The use of drinking chocolate is now highly fashionable in France, Spain, and Italy.

1657

A Frenchman opens London's first chocolate house called The Coffee Mill and Tobacco Roll. Soon, chocolate houses become fashionable meeting places where London's social players meet to drink the luxurious beverage and discuss "business affairs." By 1674, the shop is offering solid eating chocolate.

1662

Given his utter disdain for its taste, Pope Pius V decrees chocolate unacceptable to drink in 1659. But only three years later, Cardinal Brancaccio decides the exotic beverage does not break the fast, ushering in chocolate's growing popularity in Italy.

Praline — the popular almond filling — is "invented" from the wreckage of a kitchen accident involving a dropped bowl of almonds and a spilled pan of hot, burnt sugar. The literally thrown-together mixture is served to the Duke of Plesslis-Praslin, an ambassador serving King Louis XIII, who not only loves the concoction, but also gives it his name.

1671

1711

Charles VI relocates his court to Vienna from Madrid and brings his favorite treats—like chocolate—with him.

A table mill for grinding cacao is invented by Dubuisson, a Frenchman, making chocolate production easier and chocolate more affordable.

1732

1753

Cocoa is given its official botanical name of Theobroma cacao by Swedish scientist Carl von Linne.

1765

In Dorchester, Massachusetts, Dr. James Baker and John Hannon begin producing chocolate "cakes" in a converted gristmill. Intended for the making of drinking chocolate, these unsweetened cakes mark a milestone in the American chocolate industry.

1779

John Hannon, business partner in the early days of Baker's Chocolate, disappears at sea while on a bean-buying voyage to the West Indies. Dr. Baker becomes the sole proprietor of their successful chocolate business.

Casparus van Houten sets up a small, primitive cocoa mill in his house in Amsterdam. As manpower is the only utility available, the pivot of the mill is kept in motion by laborers running around in circles.

1815

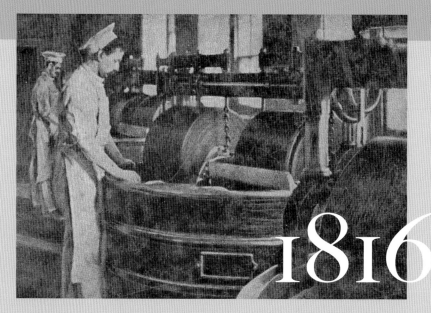

1816

Jean-Antoine Brutus Menier creates chocolate-covered medicine. Many also credit the Frenchman with building the first chocolate factory.

1824

John Cadbury opens a grocery in Birmingham, England, and, by grinding and selling his own cacao beans, lays the groundwork for the Cadbury empire.

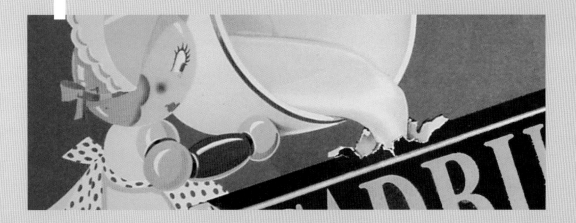

1828

Dutchman Coenraad van Houten invents the first chocolate press to extract cocoa butter from chocolate and subsequently develops cocoa powder. Soon after, in an effort to make a more mixable chocolate, he invents "Dutched cocoa."

1830

"Eating chocolate," a bitter and brittle forerunner to the modern candy bar, is invented by J. S. Fry & Sons of England. By 1847, Fry & Sons produces "Chocolat Delicieux à Manger," thought to be the first tasty chocolate bar for eating.

1849

Domingo Ghirardelli arrives in San Francisco in search of gold. Failing that, he begins selling chocolate to miners, thus beginning Ghirardelli chocolates.

Schrafft's Candy opens a small Boston store.

1861

1868

French confectioner Etienne Guittard opens a chocolate shop in San Francisco.

1872

The Baker Chocolate Company adopts Jean-Etienne Liotard's painting "La Belle Chocolatière" as its trademark, one of the oldest such trademarks in the United States.

1875

With the help of Henri Nestlé, Swiss chocolatier Daniel Peter introduces sweetened condensed milk to his chocolate recipes, resulting in the invention of milk chocolate.

1878

Maillard's chocolates are becoming the chocolates of choice for New Yorkers. Its ads proclaim that the chocolates are sold at grocers everywhere, and a Maillard's chocolate school is set up for chocolate-making instruction.

1879

In perhaps one of the most significant advances in chocolate making, Rudolph Lindt of Switzerland invents the conching machine, eliminating the inconsistencies inherent to processed chocolate and producing the smoothest chocolate yet. This chocolate "fondant" as he called it, was also the first reliable melting chocolate.

1893–1894

At the World's Columbian Exposition in Chicago, Milton Hershey marvels at German-made chocolate equipment. Purchasing the machinery, he sends it back to his caramel factory in Pennsylvania and begins producing his own chocolate: cocoa, chocolate coatings, baking chocolate, and, of course, the first Hershey bar. Also showing at the fair are Stollwerck Chocolate from Germany and Lowney's from Boston.

Schrafft's Candy opens a shop in New York's Herald Square. Soon, the little confection store serves lunch and dinner along with its acclaimed candies.

1897

1899

Rudolph Lindt sells his recipes and conching technology to David Sprüngli, marking the beginning of Swiss industry giant Lindt & Sprüngli.

1900

Hershey's first Milk Chocolate Bar is introduced.

1904

Emil J. Brach opens Brach's Palace of Sweets in Chicago.

1906

In honor of Milton Hershey, Derry Township, site of the Hershey-built chocolate factory and town, renames itself Hershey, Pennsylvania.

The Hershey's Kiss is born on July 1.

1907

Jean Tobler of Switzerland introduces the renowned Toblerone bar.

1908

Frank and Ethel Mars establish the Mars Company in Tacoma, Washington, while on the other coast, Milton Hershey reaches sales exceeding $5 million.

1911

1912

America begins eating chocolate in a whole different way as Whitman's Company introduces the first Whitman's Sampler. The sampler and its guide to what's inside will remain an American favorite for years. Whitman's is one of the first chocolatiers to sell boxed chocolates sealed in cellophane.

Swiss chocolatier Jules Sechaud invents the bon bon, the first filled chocolate.

1913

1914

In Robinson, Illinois, L. S. Heath & Sons introduces the Heath Bar, a toffee bar covered in milk chocolate.

The annual average of U.S. candy consumption per person reaches almost six pounds.

24 AMERICA'S Bars
Finest Candy BAR
English 5¢
HEATH
Toffee ~

1920

The Curtiss Candy Company of Chicago gives birth to Baby Ruth.

1921

After more that twenty years in business, Louis Sherry opens his famous chocolate and ice cream parlor on Park Avenue in New York. Louis Sherry's shops sell chocolates and treats well into the 1950s.

Using Hershey's chocolate, H. B. Reese, a former Hershey employee, creates the Reese's Peanut Butter Cup.

1922

Mr. and Mrs. Russell Stover open a candy business in their bungalow in Denver, Colorado. The company is called Mrs. Stover's Bungalow Candies and changes twenty years later to Russell Stover Candies. By 1954, it has 40 stores and its candy is sold at over 2,000 department, grocery, and drug stores.

The first Cadbury Creme Egg is introduced. However, the modern Cadbury egg we all know wasn't created until 1971.

1923

1924

Natale Olivieri of New Jersey adds Yoo-Hoo chocolate drink, in a seven-ounce bottle, to his Tru-Fruit soda line.

The New York Cocoa Exchange is established. In 1935, Gretchen Schoenleber, president of Ambrosia Chocolate Company of Milwaukee, is the first woman to join a commodity exchange, the New York Cocoa Exchange.

1926

Belgian chocolatier Joseph Draps founds the Godiva company. His wife suggests that the famous nude rider speaks to Godiva Chocolatier's target audience, as she symbolizes luxury, and decadence. Lady Godiva becomes the company's logo.

1927

General Foods buys America's first chocolate company, Baker's Chocolate.

1928

Schrafft's is now an established popular confection and restaurant chain, with twenty-nine locations in New York and four in Boston. Uniformed waitresses serve lunch, dinner, and, of course, desserts and confections.

Cella's Confections, a New York-based candy maker, begins covering cherries with chocolate. Chocolate-covered cherries, fondant style, will remain fashionable until the 1970s.

1929

1930

Having run out of baking chocolate, Ruth Wakefield instead adds chunks of a Nestlé bar to her cookie dough. By doing so, Mrs. Wakefield, proprietress of the Toll House Inn in New Bedford, Massachusetts, inadvertently creates an American classic — the chocolate chip cookie.

Mars introduces the Snickers bar. The candy bar becomes the best-selling brand in the United States.

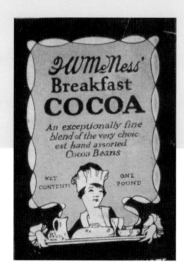

Cocoa, spice, and pure vanilla extract producer McNess gains a national reputation with first prize at the 1933–1934 Chicago World's Fair.

1934

1938

Nestlé Crunch and Hershey Krackle both enter the market offering milk chocolate infused with crisped rice bits.

Industry giant Bloomer Chocolate Company starts up in Chicago.

1939

1941

Forrest Mars teams up with Bruce Murrie, a former president of Hersheys, and establishes M&M, Ltd. Soon after, they set out to create a candy especially for American G.I.s, and M&Ms are born.

Hershey develops the Army-issue, hearty, four-ounce, Ration D chocolate bar. They are made without cocoa butter and contain a whopping 600 calories of "energy."

1942

1948

Nestlé Quik chocolate milk drink mix is introduced to compete with top-selling Ovaltine.

1954

Serendipity opens in New York and will serve customers special confections and treats for years to come. Their frozen hot chocolate drink is an instant hit.

1958

General Foods prints the recipe for the German Chocolate Cake on the box of its chocolate. The popular regional recipe combines chocolate layers with caramel and coconut and nut frosting.

1963

Hershey's buys Reese's Milk Chocolate Peanut Butter Cups from neighbor and former employee H.B. Reese.

1966

Soup is good food, but chocolate may be better: Campbell's buys Godiva Chocolatier, Inc., and soon introduces America to European-style premium chocolate, packaged in a fancy gold box.

1969

Cadbury Schweppes, Ltd., is formed when the two companies merge. Together, they form a food conglomerate producing everything from beverages to boxed chocolate.

Tobler and Suchard join forces and become one of the largest chocolate groups. Their classic chocolate products make them a huge European enterprise.

SUCHARD

1970

1973

Two chocolate theme parks open: Cadbury's Chocolate World in Birmingham, England, and Hershey's Chocolate World in Hershey, Pennsylvania.

1976

American chocolate bars increase in price from 15 to 20 cents, while in Berkeley, California, Alice Medrich opens her chocolate store, Cocolat. Medrich introduces handmade, European-style chocolates, effectively creating an American trend back toward artisinal chocolates.

1983

Nestlé buys Ward-Johnson confections, taking on classic brands Oh Henry, Goobers, Sno-Caps, and the cute, square Chunky.

Lake Champlain Chocolates owner, Jim Lampman, rolls his first truffles for patrons at his acclaimed Ice House restaurant in Burlington, Vermont.

1985

Nestlé introduces Alpine White Chocolate Bars.

1987

Frank Mars embarks on his last big business venture when he introduces Ethel M Chocolates in Las Vegas. The retailer is named for his mother and specializes in liquor-filled chocolates.

Russell Stover pays $35 million for Whitman's Chocolate's assets and trademarks from Pet Foods.

1993

Made using traditional manufacturing methods and well-blended beans, Scharffen Berger Chocolate introduces pure bittersweet chocolate. This helps set a new standard for premium chocolate in the United States.

1997

1998

Lindt & Sprüngli buys American chocolate producer Ghirardelli.

A FAVORITE SINCE 1852.

Favorites: Descriptions and Terms

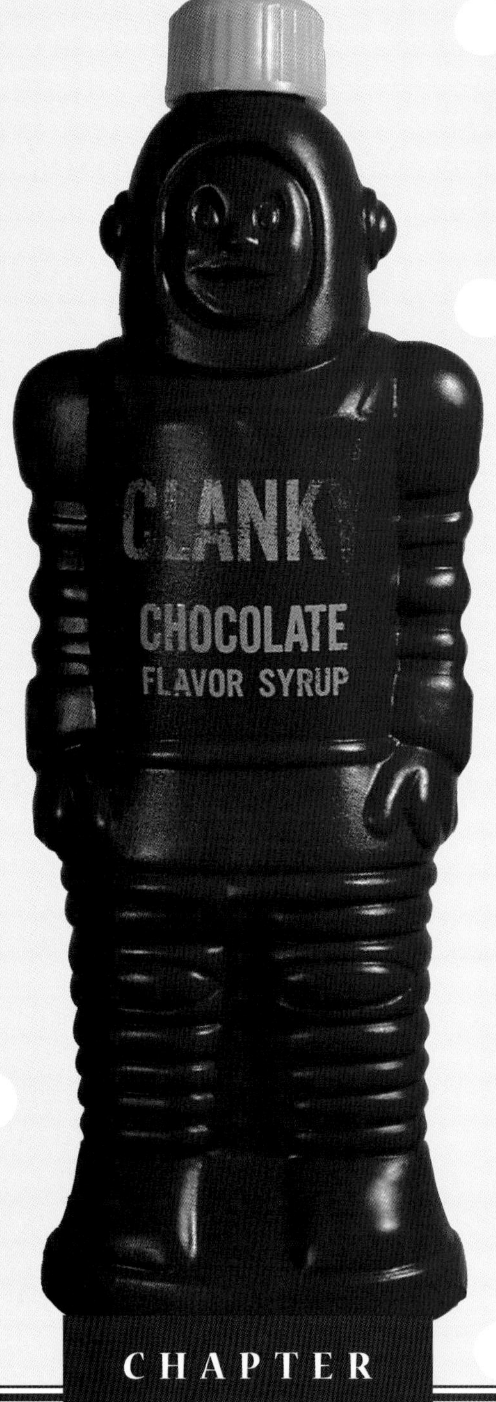
CLANKY
CHOCOLATE
FLAVOR SYRUP

CHAPTER THREE

Baking chocolate

Unsweetened chocolate formulated for desserts and chocolate work. Bitter tasting; may not be suitable for straight eating. Also known as bitter chocolate, unsweetened chocolate, or chocolate liquor.

Bar chocolate

Sweetened chocolate bars, designed solely for personal consumption and eating enjoyment, not for baking purposes. May have inclusions like peanuts in the chocolate.

Bloom

Dull, grey film or streaks that appear on the surface of chocolate. Improper storage, moisture, and/or heat can cause the fragile cocoa butter to release from the chocolate.

Cacao

The pure plant and the seeds that produce chocolate. Refers to the natural product before processing and additives are combined to form chocolate. Also refers to the tree, grown in the tropics worldwide, whose seeds are processed into chocolate. Cacao grows in humid, wet forests, sheltered by a canopy of taller trees or "mother trees."

Cacao beans

Seeds from the fruit pods of cacao trees. Approximately fifty seeds are encased in a sticky pulp in each fruit. Beans are fermented and dried and then roasted and ground to create chocolate.

Cacao nibs

The interior meat of a cacao bean separated from the outside husks; nibs are the heart of chocolate. Bakers and confectioners use them for crunchiness and subtle chocolate flavor in sweets and savory dishes.

Cacao pod

The large fruits of the cacao tree. The pods, depending on the variety, are usually zeppelin-shaped, with skin like a textured melon. Each pod contains about fifty seeds that can be processed into chocolate. Usually bright green while growing, when ripe they turn brown, yellow, or red. There are three main classifications: criollo, forastero, and trinitario.

Chocolate

Tempered food or flavoring made from the roasted seeds of the cacao tree, *Theobroma cacao*. It is used as a main ingredient and along with many confections. The word comes from the Aztec name cacahautl, meaning bitter water. Initially it was a spiced beverage, native to Venezuela, used by the Mayas and Aztecs.

Chocolate chips and morsels

Small bits of chocolate that are made with less cocoa butter and designed to work well in baking and serve decorative purposes.

Chocolate coatings and syrups

Liquid chocolate, from which cocoa butter is removed and to which vegetable oils and stabilizers are added for easy flow or application. The substitution of other fats for cocoa butter make these less expensive and easier to use than real chocolate.

Chocolate liquor

Thick, gritty paste produced from grinding roasted cacao nibs; the pure and unsweetened product of the roasted cacao seeds. There is no alcohol content in chocolate liquor. Instead, the term refers to the cocoa essence. Also called cocoa mass.

Cocoa butter

Yellowish-white vegetable fat extracted from pure chocolate liquor with high-pressure machinery. Cocoa butter has a melting point of 97 degrees Fahrenheit, close to body temperature. Edible and nutritious, with many industrial uses, it is an important ingredient in the cosmetic industry.

This precious bone-building Vitamin D... in a delicious, natural FOOD

It is really a very simple matter to understand why the fact that Vitamin D is contained in Cocomalt is so important to mothers ... to doctors ... to nutritionists.

We know that children must have this precious vitamin — for without it, the milk minerals (lime and phosphorus) in their diet which go to make strong bones and teeth are not utilized by the body.

Cod-liver oil is *one* source. The direct rays of the sun are another ... But Cocomalt offers a further advantage: it brings to your children not only the actual vitamin but the necessary milk minerals (lime and phosphorus) as well—in a delicious *natural* food that youngsters really love.

You see, milk is particularly rich in mineral salts. That's an important reason why doctors say children should drink plenty of milk. And Cocomalt not only increases the milk minerals by over half, but it also furnishes the Vitamin D which puts the minerals to work in a way that builds bones, develops sound teeth, prevents rickets (soft bones, bowed legs) and assures the steady symmetrical growth of the whole body.

More than that, Cocomalt is a completely *balanced* food. It is so rich in proteins and carbohydrates that it adds 70% more *nourishment* to milk and combines, in scientific proportions, the nourishing elements ideally suited to children ...

A DELICIOUS DRINK THAT CHILDREN REALLY LIKE

It is a particularly happy circumstance that so vital a factor in health and vigor should be found in a *balanced* food and in a truly delicious drink.

For children *do* drink Cocomalt because they *like* it. It has a delightful chocolate flavor. You can give it to them hot or cold — for breakfast, supper and after school lunch. And mothers who ordinarily find it difficult to make their children drink the daily glasses of milk they need have discovered in Cocomalt the perfect answer to this problem.

Cocomalt should, without question, be a part of every child's diet.

R. B. DAVIS COMPANY, Hoboken, N.J. • *Makers of Davis Baking Powder*

A generous sample and booklet • Send 10 cents (to cover the cost of mailing) and we will forward you a generous sample can of Cocomalt—together with a fascinating book entitled "Children of the Sun." This booklet was prepared for the R. B. Davis Company by specialists in the field of medicine and nutrition, based on their own comprehensive research work on Coco-

R.B. Davis Co., Hoboken, N.J. Enclosed find 10 cents. Send me booklet C-4 and sample of Cocomalt mentioned at left.

Name_____
Street_____
County_____
City_____

You may get Cocomalt from your grocer in half-pound, pound and five pound cans. The half-pound size is 25 cents (30 cents west of the Mississippi). If your grocer cannot supply you, take advantage of the sample offer.

Cocomalt

HOT OR COLD

Cocomalt
A Delicious Food Drink
Chocolate Flavor

© R. B. D. CO. '29

It's your wish come true in chocolate flavor!

THE EXTRA-RICH SYRUP TO "PARTIFY" MILK DRINKS... MAKE DESSERTS GORGEOUS AS THIS.

BOSCO
PRINCESS MERINGUES

(Serves 4)
8 Bosco meringue glacés
Pistachio ice cream

Stir 2 tsp. Bosco into a 2-egg basic meringue glacé. Drop spoonfuls on cookie sheet. Bake slowly (250° F.) 75 min. Leave in oven 15 min. Cool. Serve with ice cream and Bosco sauce. Here's a pride of a dessert - with chocolate flavor the way you want it! Richer ... more chocolaty! For Bosco is delicious extra-strength! It's time-saving and economical ... the chocolate flavoring for frostings, puddings, cakes. Bosco tastes grand in hot or cold milk ... adds Iron and Vitamin D! Get Bosco at your grocer's ... be sure of finest quality in chocolate-flavored syrup!

BOSCO

THRILLING SHOW! Tune in "Land of the Lost" Saturday mornings, A.B.C. Network

BOSCO
Milk Amplifier

A DELICIOUS CHOCOLATE-MALT FLAVORED SYRUP
NET WEIGHT 1½ LBS.

BOSCO is made from Cocoa, Barley Malt, Sugar and Artificial (vanilla) flavoring and is fortified with Vitamin D (Produced by the activation of Ergosterol), and biologically available Iron.

BOSCO COMPANY, INC. - NEW YORK, N.Y.

Cocoa became a preferred breakfast drink for children and was used to flavor drinks. Because of its flavor appeal it was often enhanced with vitamins.
Courtesy Michael Rosenberg Collection

Cocoa percentage

The percentage amount of chocolate liquor that is included in a formula. A higher cocoa content has a stronger flavor and less sugar. Cocoa percentage does not indicate quality.

Cocoa powder

A powder with its creamy cocoa butter removed. Made by pressing the pure chocolate liquor at very high pressure to produce a defatted powder.

Conching

A technique invented by Rudolph Lindt that stirs chocolate with rotating, shell-shaped mixers to create a smooth texture.

Couverture

French term for a chocolate formula with a higher cocoa butter content than a standard eating bar. The high cocoa butter content contributes to fluidity, ease of handling, and creation of finished chocolate with high-gloss and velvety taste.

Criollo

The native Venezuelan variety of the *Theobroma* cacao plant, which accounts for 10 percent of all commercial cacaos. Produces very fine-grade chocolate with a pure flavor. This delicate variety, however, produces fewer pods with less seeds and is not as hardy as other varieties.

In 1863, Gerardus Johannes Droste opened his shop in Haarlem, Holland, where he served hot chocolate and small eating chocolates he called Pastilles Droste. By 1891, he was producing cocoa and chocolate on a large scale, and his products entered the American market in 1905 with this packaging showing typical Dutch farm children.
Courtesy Beth Kimmerle Collection

Known for tasty taffy-like treats, Tootsie Roll expanded its brand into prepared fudge mixes in the 1930s to capitalize on its chocolate stronghold.
Courtesy Michael Rosenberg Collection

Dark chocolate

General term for chocolate that is made from a combination of chocolate liquor, cocoa butter, sugar, and vanilla. Dark chocolate bars have above 50 percent chocolate content.

Dutch-processed cocoa powder

Refers to an alkaline treatment of the cocoa liquor. This process darkens the cocoa and modifies the chocolate flavor, helping to neutralize natural acidity and bitterness.

Fair Trade

Certified method of production and plantation management which assures that the workers who grow and harvest the raw cacao product are treated well and fairly compensated. Also requires that environmental standards be adhered to.

Filled chocolate

These various styles are commonly referred to as "boxed chocolates," truffles, or bon bons. They have centers that are dipped, encased, or enrobed in chocolate. Popular centers include caramel, cream, fondants, gianduja with hazelnut, nougat, praline, and ganache.

Forastero

Most common variety of *Theobroma cacao* pods, accounting for 80 percent of all commercial cocoa. The hearty pods grow well but produce below-average chocolate with poor flavor. Most forastero beans are blended with other beans by chocolatiers to create a flavor profile or recipe.

Ganache

Traditional filling of many truffles. Ganache is a simple chocolate mixture that combines heated cream and chocolate.

Hot chocolate

Originally made with ground cocoa stirred or mixed with boiling water. Today, it is usually made with cocoa powder and sugar, combined with heated milk.

Lecithin

Natural emulsifier derived from egg yolks and legumes — usually soybeans. It helps maintain an emulsion or attachment between cocoa butter and sugar during the chocolate-making process.

Milk chocolate

Chocolate made from a combination of chocola liquor, cocoa butter, sugar, vanilla, and milk or cream. Milk chocolate contains at least 10 perce chocolate liquor and at least 12 percent total mi ingredients. It is softer and milder than a dark chocolate, often with cream and caramel notes.

Molded chocolate

Hollow or solid piece that starts as liquid chocolate, that is tempered and poured into a mold. Once cooled, chocolate will take the exact shape of th mold form. Also known as moulded.

Organic

Method of agriculture that respects the soil in which plants are grown. Farms and plantations using organic methods do not use chemicals or sprays, including pesticides and chemical fertilizers, in farming, thereby producing clean and organically grown produce.

Semisweet and bittersweet chocolate

Chocolate made from a combination of chocola liquor, cocoa butter, vanilla, and sugar, but containing at least 35 percent chocolate liquor. Bittersweet chocolate and semisweet chocolate are often called dark chocolate.

Single origin

Chocolates made from beans from a single source, country, or region. Also known as grand cru, single-origin chocolates are gaining recognition, as most chocolates are the results of blending several beans from different growing regions. Blending beans can balance taste qualities: mild, acidic, fruity, or earthy. As single-origin chocolate is from one source, it is a challenge to produce a consistent end product.

Tempering

The heating, cooling, and reheating of chocolate in order to stabilize the cocoa butter crystals. Liquid chocolate must stay within precise temperatures to be properly tempered. Tempered chocolate, when cooled and hardened, creates shine as well as a proper snap, and is necessary for molding candy, and coating work.

Trinitero

Variety of the cocoa plant, a type of *Theobroma cacao*, accounting for 10 percent all commercial cocoa. The bean is a hybrid of criollo and forastero, grown primarily in the Caribbean. Produces a fine-grade bean with a spicy, complex flavor.

Vanilla

Tropical orchid plant native to Mexico that produces an edible pod used to make fragrant flavor and extract. Often used to heighten the flavor of other ingredients, the vanilla pod or bean can be cured and macerated in alcohol for a liquid extract form.

Vanillin

Artificial ingredient made from wood-pulp byproducts. Vanillin is used in chocolate to enhance the flavor; it is also used as a substitute for vanilla.

White chocolate

Technically, not really chocolate, as it contains no chocolate liquor or solids. Is also called "confectioner's coating." This is a product made from cocoa butter, milk, and sugar. In 2002, the FDA established a standard for white chocolate. Better white chocolate contains at least 20 percent cocoa butter and 14 percent total milk ingredients, while in cheaper coatings, cocoa butter is replaced by vegetable fats.

**CHAPTER
FOUR**

Eline's

Milwaukee's Schlitz Brewing Company created Eline's Chocolate. It was the popular Midwestern brewer's effort to produce a beneficial and wholesome product at a time when America's attitudes toward alcohol-based beverages were changing drastically.

Schlitz anticipated that the brewing industry was susceptible to social disapproval. As early as 1916 some of Milwaukee's temperate teetotalers were looking for change. The "nondrinkers" pointed out that, in 1889, brewing was Milwaukee's largest industry and that one-twentieth of all goods produced in the city in 1915 was beer; it was a number too large for their liking.

In 1919, soon after Prohibition went into effect, the Schlitz Brewing Company was forced to cease beer-making operations. During the fourteen-year dry spell, president Alfred Uihlein sought profitable substitutes to brewing beer, meanwhile continuing to hope that the Prohibition law would be repealed. The company experimented with various business ventures, including the Eline Milk Chocolate Bar operation.

Many believed that, with beer and liquor outlawed, the public would turn to the socially acceptable indulgences of chocolate, ice cream, and candies. They were correct. As bars and clubs closed, ice cream parlors, soda fountains, and candy stores quickly set up and thrived.

But, instead of starting a new business in a straightforward manner, the Uihlein family built a huge chocolate plant, attempting to rival Hershey's Pennsylvania factory. Both were located in the heart of American dairy farmland. Joseph, Sr. enthusiastically announced, "Wisconsin is the greatest dairy state in the union and good fresh milk is the one requirement for a chocolate manufacturer . . . . We have made plans for unlimited expansion."

The overbuilt Milwaukee Eline factory lobby was paved with Italian marble, each office had a working fireplace, the garage was built from historic European architectural plans, and the entrance pillars were modeled on Stanford White designs. In building Eline's Chocolate, no expenses were spared; confectionary experts were brought in and elaborate plans for developing and marketing new chocolate products were prepared.

The story soon became bittersweet. The Uihleins brewed better beer than they created creamy chocolate.

The chocolate plan experienced a variety of

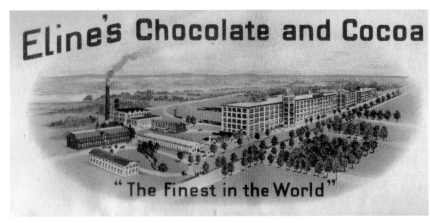

59

production and formula problems, but the intrepid Uihleins were slow to admit that they were in over their heads. Chocolate was simply harder to make, store, and ship than their beer that made Milwaukee famous.

By 1924, rumors circulated that the massive plant was for sale. But the Uihleins persevered, continuing to invest millions of dollars in additional labor and machinery, as well as expanding into more confectionary product lines. Colossal budgets were spent on promotional products to attract customers. Eline's even distributed an Eline's dictionary to schools and clubs in the Midwest to remind children to ask for Eline's chocolate and cocoa; the targeted audience never heard the call.

The Eline Milk Chocolate Bar venture was discontinued in 1928. The family finally decided it had lost enough. A total of $17 million was dumped in the ill-fated and over-ambitious chocolate extravaganza.

Despite the candy venture setback, Schlitz Brewing survived the dry Prohibition years by becoming involved in some wise investments and the manufacturing of malt syrup for cooking, the baking, and soft drinks. On April 7, 1933, Prohibition ended for beer. Only 160 out of more than a thousand small local breweries survived the dry years. Schlitz Brewing remained in chocolate but only as a powder additive supplier for "malted" milk shakes.

The Eline's factory will be remembered for producing the chocolate that was never famous, made by the family that went, as the old Schlitz slogan declared, "for the gusto."

Deliciously Good

Cocoa Syrup

With the onset of Prohibition, many beer producers scrambled to find businesses that would keep them afloat while they attempted to repeal laws that made liquor illegal. Although seemingly more delicious, Eline's, the short lived, Schlitz-owned chocolate brand, never caught on like malt liquor.
Courtesy Beth Kimmerle Collection

Iced Cocoa

Fanny Farmer Candies

Before Martha Stewart, and even before Julia Child, there was Fannie Merritt Farmer. Born on March 23, 1857, in Boston, Massachusetts, she grew up in nearby Medford. During her high school years Fannie suffered a stroke and was forced to discontinue her education. Although she slowly recovered from the stroke, she was considered an "unfit" potential bride and never married. She went to work instead as a "mother's assistant," and it was in the kitchens of her employees where she developed an aptitude for home cooking.

With her parents' support, Fannie Farmer studied cooking under Mary J. Lincoln at the Boston Cooking School, which was known for its reputable classes teaching cooking of standard American fare and adaptations of European-based "Continental cuisine."

While teaching at the school, Lincoln published her gastronomical guide, Boston Cooking-School Cook Book, aimed at cooking schools as a training tool for professional cooks.

Interestingly, the rising middle class with expendable income, together with many women who aspired to make homemaking their profession, found the Boston cookbook helpful. Fannie Farmer graduated from Lincoln's school in 1889 and remained there as assistant director, becoming headmistress in 1894.

Fannie Farmer revised and reissued the recognized cookbook in 1896, adding many improvements. The principal innovation was her standardization of measurements for every recipe, making the final results dependable and consistent. Fannie's cookbook was a huge hit, and later it was translated into many languages. It revolutionized both cooking and recipe writing. Before her cookbook, ingredient lists were estimates and amounts were often referred to as a pinch, handful, or dash. With a no-nonsense approach, the book made domestic living easier for ordinary housewives. To date, the Fannie Farmer cookbook has sold more than three million copies.

In 1902, she opened her very own Miss Farmer's School of Cookery, aimed at training middle-class American housewives in cookery. She was a frequent lecturer on domestic subjects and a pioneer in the field of nutrition and diet planning. She wrote several more cooking-related books before she died in Boston in 1915. Her namesake school continued until 1944. However, her chocolates carried on much longer.

Frank O'Connor came to the United States from Canada in 1919 to start an American candy company. He wanted his company to reflect quality ingredients, freshness, and high standards. He soon realized that Fannie Merritt Farmer's image was perfect for his line of chocolates. Fannie's name symbolized the essence of exacting care and time-

tested recipes. Her cookbook was used in millions of homes, and she was admired for her courage in fighting her personal physical hardship. She had the perfect persona for a box of kitchen-fresh confections.

Frank opened his first Fanny Farmer Candies shop on Main Street in Rochester, New York. He altered the spelling of Fannie's name, however, to avoid competition with the recently opened Fannie May stores. He styled the first store to resemble the interior of a comfy new home, with frilly curtains and a warm welcoming staff. The inviting store was clean and white, with simple touches like a Fanny Farmer signature sign located above the door. With a miniature lighthouse that blinked a hospitable, safe-haven hello, the store beckoned customers to try Fanny Farmer's chocolate treats.

Customers could purchase one-pound Fanny Farmer boxes hand-packed with their favorite chocolate assortments. A frame of her trusty and sturdy face adorned the top of the candy box lid. One side portrayed the symbolic Statue of Liberty, offset by a picturesque image of an ideal house titled "The Homestead." This signature box was used into the 1960s.

Frank's Fanny Farmer Chocolate store concept was an immediate success. Fanny Farmer shops were opened in other East Coast cities with the same décor, fresh candy, and friendly atmosphere.

Before the advent of electric refrigeration in 1937, professional confectioners used fresh ingredients to produce Fanny Farmer candy in studios or off-site kitchens that supplied several local shops in an area. This technique insured fresh product at every new location. Fanny Farmer continued to grow throughout the Depression years of the 1930s and the war years of the 1940s.

During World War II, necessary ingredients, such as sugar, were rationed and in short supply. But Fanny Farmer Chocolates continued to make what they could while supporting the war efforts by mailing assortments to servicemen around the world.

The company remained an East Coast confection favorite for years and stayed solid throughout the sixties. The arrival of fancy European boxed chocolate companies left little room for the classic American standards, however. Fanny Farmer stores closed one by one until the Archibald Candy Corporation purchased the fifty that remained in 1992. In its halcyon days of the 1990s, Archibald was the largest retail candy company in the United States and operated hundreds of retail Fannie May, Fanny Farmer, and Canada-based Laura Secord shops.

Fanny Farmer

NET WEIGHT
7 ½ OZS.

WHOLESOME SWEETS FOR CHILDREN

1940s packaging. The Fanny Farmer name had just the right
sound for a start-up chocolate company. Fannie Merrit Farmer
was a turn-of-the-century cooking maven who's name was subtly
skewed for this classic American confectioner.
Courtesy Michael Rosenberg Collection

Louis Sherry

In 1881, popular caterer and confectioner Louis Sherry opened his first candy shop and restaurant at 662 Sixth Avenue in New York City. By 1890, Mr. Sherry opened a more serious establishment, a fancy restaurant on Fifth Avenue and 37th Street. Sherry's fine and fancy friends and clients spread the word about his delicious products, and they confirmed his success from the outset. The restaurant quickly became the site for private aristocratic balls and suppers hosted by New York's wealthy and privileged elite.

On the first floor was his immensely popular chocolate and confectionary shop while down in the basement he established an area for ice cream and pastry production, along with a general kitchen. Louis Sherry's personal living quarters were located on the second floor above the establishment. He was a true artisan confectioner and maintained, "From the start I was determined not to let anything out of my house that was not made in the best possible way and out of the best and most expensive materials available in the market." For years, Sherry's superior specialties were served to the likes of financier J. P. Morgan and social doyenne Lady Astor.

In 1898, Sherry's moved uptown to the increasingly fashionable Upper East Side. The restaurant became increasingly popular and prosperous. Theodore Dreiser referred to it in Sister Carrie, writing that the dining room is "the place where the matter of expense limited the patrons to the moneyed or pleasure-loving class." Edith Wharton mentioned Sherry's in several passages of House of Mirth. Her character, Lawrence Seldon, says to the main character, Lily Bart, "Shall we go over to Sherry's for a cup of tea?" She responds, "I'm dying for a tea — but isn't there a quieter place?" His restaurant became more prosperous and stylish than ever, making him a wealthy and confident confectioner and restaurateur. At the zenith of the Gilded Age, Sherry's hosted elaborate consumption celebrations — a turn-of-the-century temple of gastronomy.

On May 17, 1919, after forty years of producing fine chocolates and foods, Louis Sherry sold his business and retired to Europe. As Sherry was a man of merriment and bubbly beverages, he was deeply disturbed by the coming dry era of Prohibition. Sherry's confectionary operation lived on and was moved to another high-profile location, the corner of Fifth Avenue and 48th Street in New York City.

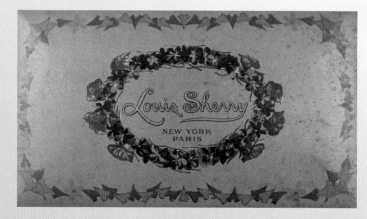

Louis Sherry's thoughtful attention to quality passed to his successors, and his confections were firmly established with support from advertisements that touted, "When it's a matter of taste . . . Louis Sherry." Before long, more confectionary shops and restaurants were named in Sherry's honor and rose in prominent locations around Manhattan. Sherry's signature handmade creations were produced in Long Island City where the company could hand-package factory-fresh chocolates in elegant, lavender-ribbon-tied boxes and tins.

The wealthy, retired confectioner and ice cream magnate then went on to succeed in another remarkable project. With Lucius Boomer, he developed Manhattan's elegant Sherry-Netherland residence hotel in 1927. Still located on the corner of Fifth Avenue and 59th Street, the Sherry-Netherland Hotel remains one of the more magic and romantic buildings in New York City. It sits opposite the Grand Army Plaza, which marks the East Side gateway to Central Park. When it welcomed its first guests, the building was the world's tallest apartment-hotel, and its vaulted lobby remains discretely lavish. The base of the building is adorned with fantastic griffins clutching bronze lanterns, while the top of the structure boasts an elaborate tower with an elegant copper minaret. It is a successful combination of

1950s Sherry's advertisement. Louis Sherry was a classic New York confectioner and businessman who went on to build the beautiful Fifth Avenue landmark, The Sherry Netherland Hotel. Courtesy New York Public Library

romance, originality, and location in keeping with the high standards Louis Sherry maintained in all his projects.

Louis Sherry's tasty legacy lives on as Louis Sherry Brands of Chicago, which sells preserves and ice cream. They are still available in very select locations in Eastern seaboard cities.

LOWNEY'S CHOCOLATE HERMITS
Plate XV.   For Receipt see page 275

COCOA ICE CREAM
Plate XVII.   For Receipt see page 298

CHOCOLATE MOUSSE
Plate XVIII.   For Receipt see page 298

Lowney's

The 1893 Columbian Exposition in Chicago provided a stunning showcase for America's industrial advancements. Established entrepreneurs showed off their best new wares and products. Eager onlookers viewed the advancements with hope, awe, and amazement; some were potential customers and some were simply spies in the house of industry. It was a challenge — a call for innovation with displays set up by category — often with direct competitors facing off with one another. The Columbian Exposition gave American chocolate a kick-start.

It was here that Boston cocoa purveyor Walter M. Lowney exhibited the first set of primitive American chocolate bars. Englishman J. S. Fry had already formulated a version but had not perfected it, and, additionally, it was unsuitable for import into the United States. Along with its early and exciting rendition of eating chocolate, Lowney's Chocolate sponsored an entire pavilion displaying hand-filled bon bons. Lowney's had been thriving in the chocolate business for a number of years before setting up in Chicago. For six months, the elaborate Lowney's Chocolate Pavilion crowned the show.

But unbeknownst to Lowney's, a certain scout combed the halls, looking at machinery and exploring the potential of chocolate. Milton Hershey quickly ordered new chocolate bar machinery and converted his prosperous Pennsylvania caramel factory to chocolate production.

And while Lowney's popular print advertisements, endorsed by actresses like Sarah Bernhardt, depicted smiling beauties dangling tempting treats between their elegant fingers, Milton forged ahead. Hershey soon was producing a consistent and relatively inexpensive chocolate bar.

In 1906, Lowney built a factory in Montreal, Canada, perhaps in an attempt to move his weakening business to a less saturated market. By then, Hershey, who had seen Lowney's glorious exhibit years earlier, virtually owned the North American chocolate business.

Around 1908, still well known on the Eastern seaboard for its confections, Lowney's published a cookbook by Maria Willett Howard. The book claimed she was, "… (one of) the most experienced and successful teachers of cooking in the country." The recipe book, possibly inspired by the success of Fannie Farmer's cookbook, was illustrated with color plates and came complete with additional pages advertising Lowney's top products. It was a "guide for the housekeeper, especially intended as a full record of delicious dishes sufficient for any well-to-do family …." Apparently, producing the book was a last-ditch effort to stay in a business that was becoming increasingly competitive.

Lowney's exhibited its fine chocolates at the 1893 Colombian Exposition in Chicago. Its display offered Lowney's bon bons and chocolate bars to attendees, who could also taste Juicy Fruit Gum, Cracker Jack, a hamburger, or Pabst beer — all on display for the first time at the legendary fair.
Courtesy Beth Kimmerle Collection

Lowney soon became totally immersed with Canada's ways. By 1924, he had defected to Canada entirely. His company continued to produce some candy bars into the early 1930s but was virtually unknown in the United States by the 1950s. Once a chocolate powerhouse with a remarkable and memorable trademark pavilion, the company faded into oblivion.

69

Founded in Boston in the nineteenth century, Schrafft's shops soon became renowned for the quality of their chocolates, candies, ice creams, and pastries. During its 1950s zenith, Schrafft's had over fifty stores in New York City and Boston.
Courtesy Beth Kimmerle Collection

Schrafft's

Founded in 1861 by W. F. Schrafft, this American chocolate company expanded during Boston's candy boom era of the late 1800s. Its first location was a small shop financed by Mrs. Schrafft's brother. The shop's many patrons were pleased to purchase Schrafft's famous fruit gumdrops to send to Union soldiers during the Civil War.

Business went so well that William Schrafft soon employed a young salesman, Frank Shattuck, who went on to open additional Schrafft's retail stores along the East Coast. Schrafft's built its first New York City location in 1898 in Herald Square, where the famous Macy's department store is now located. By 1928, the chain was considered vast with thriving, well-stocked stores — twenty-nine in the New York area and four in Boston.

Firmly established as a chocolate challenger, Schrafft's built the nation's largest candy factory that same year. Located in Charlestown just outside Boston, the company built an enormous facility, where more than 1,500 employees could produce handmade, boxed chocolate, fudge, and candy bars. Schrafft's was best known for its boxed chocolates, but soon the empire grew to include ice cream and a chain of popular family restaurants.

By 1950, there were more than fifty stores going strong throughout New York's five boroughs, and the company produced a variety of chocolate, ice cream, and candy bars. But by the early 1960s, mass-produced candy bars started squeezing boxed chocolates off the shelves. Less expensive boxed chocolate brands, like Russell Stover and Whitman's, were gaining market share along with higher-priced fancy European imports. Schrafft's chocolates were stuck somewhere in the unmarketable middle, and the company was ensnared in old-fashioned business ways.

Eventually, the Schrafft family sold the business, and it went into a nasty downward spiral. A series of new owners and presidents tried unsuccessfully to revive the outdated product line and solve ugly manufacturing problems. Tragically, the classic company was saddled with enormous debt by the 1970s. Schrafft's executives made an effort to purchase the company in 1984, but the owners decided to finally put the business to bed and sell off the few remaining assets. The last Schrafft's restaurant closed in 1985. Today, the phantom of the former 900,000-square-foot factory, complete with clocktower and faded Schrafft's logo, can still be glimpsed off of I-93 when traveling through Boston.

AT THE CHOCOLATE FACTORY

How Chocolate is Made

CHAPTER
FIVE

A factory is a magical place, where the dried seeds of cacao pods are transformed into ready-to-eat chocolate; witnessing the process is a treat for all the senses. A factory is often a well-conducted symphony of man-made machinery, making music with a natural object in various states: organic, liquid, solid, hot, or cold. The final outcome, be it bars or cocoa powder, seems like an impossible feat. When we witness the entire process, we gain an appreciation of the complexity of the accomplishment.

Chocolate-producing factories are relatively rare. Only nine companies in the United States purchase cacao beans and produce actual finished chocolate. There are many thousands that buy the finished chocolate to make confections; they are called "coaters." A company like M&M Mars does not sell finished chocolate for others to use; instead, it consumes and controls all the chocolate the factory produces. Still, there are others that only process and produce chocolate for large food and candy manufacturers to purchase, and they produce no consumer products. You'll never see a candy bar made by these companies, but they may produce the chip in your favorite cookie or the mocha syrup at your coffeehouse.

The fact that so few companies are involved in the refinement of cacao may be perplexing. The U.S. chocolate industry alone is valued at $13 billion dollars, but producing chocolate is an incredibly risky endeavor. Cacao is an internationally traded commodity, its price fluctuation based on world economics and our dear, fickle Mother Nature. Most cocoa is grown in poor, third-world countries, leaving the buyer open to political and economic uncertainties of sometimes unstable and unpredictable markets.

Despite these challenges, a whopping $435 million worth of beans are imported into the United States each year. Billions of beans make the trip, traveling in burlap bags printed with the plantation name, the country of origin, and the total net weight, usually around 150 pounds. They make the journey on huge freighters that hold hundreds of 90-foot containers filled with imported products.

Once the cacao beans arrive from their tropical growing regions, production facilities check and sort them. This insures that no foreign particles, parasites, or molds have arrived with the shipment. It also gives the company a chance to look at what it bought, sometimes years earlier, as cacao is traded as a future.

1950s collectible trading cards, distributed by Jacques Superchocolat of Belgium, depict the process of chocolate growing and production. (Right) Once dried, Cacao beans are transported in jute bags to storage. (Far right) Beans are stored in jute bags in preparation for travel.
Courtesy Beth Kimmerle Collection

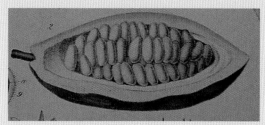

After the raw cacao beans are inspected, they are roasted. The smell of roasting is wonderful and intoxicating, but after a visit to a large factory, it is something you'll contend with for a while. Clothes, notebooks, and camera equipment may smell like roasting for weeks following. However, the scent of beans roasting is truly delicious and, if you close your eyes, you can conjure up an image of a bittersweet dark chocolate bar. The total roasting time depends on the type of bean and the quality. Beans that are of lower quality get a slower cook, as they tend to be bitter with flavors that are best to mask. On average, it will take anywhere between 20 to 30 minutes at 230 degrees Fahrenheit to complete the heating process. The beans will change to a deep brown color and begin to look like a plump, roasted almond.

The cooked beans move on to be winnowed. The outer casing or skins are removed, leaving the precious inner seed or nib. This process is much like separating wheat kernels from chaff. The shed by-product goes on to mulch makers and very low-quality "chocolate" companies. I always imagine that the chocolate companies that use this material produce items that taste like the brown bark bits from a children's playground.

What remains are the miniscule nibs, the true heart of chocolate. The crunchy nibs are usually blended together to company specifications and to insure consistent chocolate quality. Most companies blend several types of beans from different regions to get their signature "recipe." This is difficult flavor work that takes years of training, much like blending grape varietals to arrive at perfect wine blends. Nibs are also available to pastry chefs and home cooks, and some new chocolate bars even contain them, embedded in dark chocolate for a brittle and bitter cocoa surprise.

In the factory, nibs are typically ground into a fine paste called cocoa liquor. This contains no alcohol as the name might imply. It is a mass of cocoa butter fat and the crushed nibs. Finer producers leave the cocoa butter in their chocolate while others, perhaps not as concerned with quality and taste, will remove the cocoa butter to sell to cosmetic companies and other food processors. Vegetable fats and other stabilizers are common economical substitutes. Stabilizers work to keep chocolate from changes over time due to processing, storage, or use.

The cocoa liquor goes on to be mixed with other ingredients to produce finished chocolate products. Sugar, vanilla, and perhaps lecithin are commonly added to most dark chocolates. Lecithin is a natural emulsifier that is derived from soybeans, and it helps the ingredients bond. Quality dark chocolate will contain 20 to 30 percent sugars, while some overly sweet types use up to 80 percent. If a chocolate ingredient list states that it contains vanilla, it's real vanilla extract.

(Right, background) Cacao pickers, circa 1900.
Courtesy New York Public Library

(Left) Scharffen Berger's expert chocolatiers use a melangeur to mix and blend chocolate with ingredients like vanilla and sugar.
Courtesy Scharffen Berger Chocolates

Vanilla is the most popular flavor in the world. Like chocolate, it was introduced to the Europeans after the Spanish found it widely used in Mexico, often in their frothy cocoa beverage. The extract comes from the vanilla bean, technically another pod, which is the only edible fruit-bearing orchid. It makes perfect sense that chocolate and vanilla live together, as both ingredients hail from the same tropical regions and have intense, distinctive flavors that come from seeds in pods. Wonderful together, chocolate and vanilla make a prefect pairing.

Vanillin is imitation vanilla, an artificial ingredient made from wood-pulp by-products. The difference between vanilla and vanillin is remarkable; the fake version falls very flat. It smells like a cheap lip gloss combined with an air freshener. The taste is worse; a faint trace of soapy, barely spicy flavor lingers through the alcohol. Additionally, milk chocolate contains milk or cream. Good ingredients make good chocolate.

The chocolate liquor is ultimately conched for smoothness and to mellow its bitterness. Swiss chocolatier Rodolfe Lindt invented the conching process in 1880, utilizing shell-shaped rollers to grind the tiny chocolate particles. The process can take hours or days, depending on the recipe. Concerned companies take their time, and the outcome is apparent in the balanced taste and silky texture. Often, cocoa butter is added back to give the finished chocolate a smooth finish.

From there, the thick, liquid chocolate is stored in large tanks until the mix is ready to be molded or extruded into chips. Chocolate must be tempered, heated, and slightly cooled before it's ready to pour and cool completely. Once shaped, it leaves the factory to go directly to stores, pastry chefs, candy coaters, or distributors. It also may sit in a liquid state for a short time before being shipped for processing elsewhere.

Watching the chocolate-making process happen is amazing. I have been in several chocolate-producing facilities: tasting nibs, surrounded by the scent of roasting beans, mesmerized by conching machines, listening to purring tempering vats, and finally, embracing a finished chocolate bar.

As I write, Tim Burton is remaking the film version of the children's favorite *Charlie and the Chocolate Factory*. A whole new generation will be turned onto the book, cocoa, and chocolate factories. I am pleased for future candy aficionados, cooks, and chocolatiers who will witness the interior of a factory, albeit one fabricated by the creative genius of Burton. I am sure many will become inspired to be the next chocolate music makers and the cocoa dreamers of dreams.

(Above and top right) 1950s collectible trading cards, distributed by Jacques Superchocolat of Belgium, depict the process of chocolate growing and production. Once in the factory, beans get hulled and ground to make cacao liquor, or mass, which is then mixed to make chocolate bars or powder. Courtesy Beth Kimmerle Collection

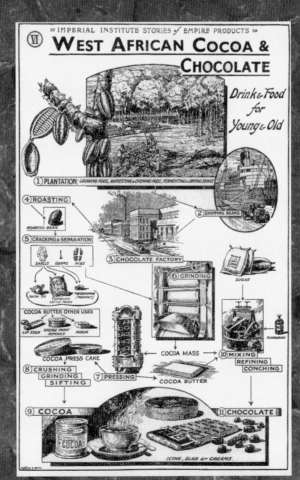

Africa's Gold Coast is the largest cacao-growing region today. This 1952 catalog page tells the story British Empire products cocoa and chocolate — "drink and food for young and old."
Courtesy Beth Kimmerle Collection

PIECE-BY-PIECE

The Chocolatiers

CHAPTER SIX

Asher's Chocolates, Inc.

Asher's candy-making company was established in 1892 when Chester A. Asher moved from Canada to Philadelphia and started his business in the heart of Germantown in the center of the city.

As Asher's grew, the firm moved to several locations in Pennsylvania. Finally, the business was consolidated and settled in Souderton, Pennsylvania; its headquarters are still located there. Chester Asher passed his knowledge and business on to his four sons, who ran the business until 1966, and they passed the business on to their children. Asher's remains in the family, with four generations of chocolate-making behind its success.

Many of Asher's chocolates are traditional favorites such as chocolate-covered pretzels, potato chips, and graham crackers; pecan-caramel patties; milk-chocolate macadamia paws; and dark-chocolate orange peels. Visitors can participate in self-guided media tours of the manufacturing plant and purchase products at its Victorian candy store. Each September, Asher's invites neighbors and customers to its fall festival at 80 Wambold Road in Stouderton.

Chester Asher, circa 1898.
Courtesy Asher's Chocolate

(Middle) Original Germantown store in the early 1900s.
(Bottom) Asher Chocolate Store 1950s. Courtesy Asher's Chocolate

79

Baker's Chocolate

How the Harvard-educated Dr. James Baker met young Irishman John Hannon is a bit of a mystery. We do know that whatever the circumstances were, Dr. Baker was able to extract a very promising piece of information — the Irishman knew how to make chocolate, a sweet treat colonists of 1764 would pay for quite handsomely. The doctor was interested in the possibilities of producing chocolate, as he regularly prescribed it for clients from his local apothecary.

Maybe even more promising for such a collaboration was that Hannon knew how to construct and operate a mill. At the time, colonists had to hand-grind and mill the cacao beans themselves, using a metate or concave stone. Many in New England had tried unsuccessfully to set up large-scale chocolate-making facilities. Though Dr. Baker was a business man eager to explore the chocolate business, the Irishman was an elusive character; not much was known about his past. So, when the transformation of a sawmill on the banks of the Neponset River was completed, the good Doctor might have looked on, somewhat nervously, as John Hannon poured cocoa beans between the stone wheels. What happened next was the stuff Baker's Chocolate is made of; the beans were pulverized to a thick liquid, which were then cooled and molded into chocolate cakes. The first large-scale American chocolate-making facility was set in motion.

This bitter chocolate concoction was purchased by colonists who then chopped it into shavings and boiled it in water for a hearty brew of sweetened cocoa. As business thrived, Dr. Baker moved up the river to a larger structure, a former cloth mill, which he rented from his brother-in-law. The doctor expanded his operation again in 1772, opening a second mill in Dorchester, Massachusetts. Rumor had it that the two partners, Hannon and Dr. Baker, were soon at odds with each other. Although they were still officially partners, Hannon opened a mill on his own to help supply the growing chocolate demand. The War for Independence had made things difficult for both chocolatiers, as the Royal Navy often troubled their incoming ships of West Indies cocoa beans.

Curiously, in 1779, Hannon reportedly disappeared on a bean-buying run to the West Indies. Some say he died in a shipwreck; others say he went missing to get away from his wife. She inherited her husband's mill, but in a short time, Dr. Baker bought her out. He consolidated the various mills into one and watched as the cacao cash poured in.

Near the beginning of the new century, Dr. Baker's son Edward took over the business and, in 1806, the new president opened a state-of-the-art chocolate mill. In an effort to grow and diversify the business, he also opened cloth and gristmills. These two mills kept the Bakers in business during the tumultuous War of 1818, as once again the English navy intercepted ships containing cacao cargo, effectively closing down the chocolate mill for nearly two years. Postwar years saw Edward tearing down his old mill in order to make a bigger and better one, which stood three stories high. By the 1830s, Edward's son Walter was running things; the new blood made some bold decisions, including adding women to his workforce. By this time, the fabulous Baker boys had competition. The brother-in-law, who had originally rented a mill to James, started his own chocolate mill, and another competitor, Webb and Twombley, set up shop on the Neponsett River as well. So thick was the chocolate smog from cocoa roasters that the area was dubbed "Chocolate Village." Walter died in 1852, ending the Baker boy reign. One hundred years after it began, the chocolate business, with its "La Belle Chocolatière" image by Jean-Etienne Liotard continued as the top-selling chocolate product in the United States. Today, the Dutch maiden remains one of the oldest product trademarks.

General Foods bought the Baker chocolate factory in 1927 and moved it from Massachusetts to Dover, Delaware, in 1965. Baker's is now part of Kraft, who merged with General Foods in 1989. Amazingly, throughout years and assorted owners, Baker's Chocolate brand has stayed true to its origin.

In the beginning, Baker's Chocolate was a seller of unsweetened chocolate bricks, or bars. These products were intended for use in making cocoa or other chocolate-flavored treats. It's almost too ironic that a man named Baker started America's baking-chocolate industry.

Pages from 1915 Baker's Recipe book. In 1883, Walter Baker & Co. adopted its famous trademark, based on La Belle Chocolatiere by Swiss artist Jean Etienne Liotard. Jean's model was Anna Baltauf, the daughter of a knight who lived in Vienna. In the mid-eighteenth century, Anna was a chocolate server in one of the city's fashionable chocolate shops. One afternoon, the Austrian Prince Ditrichstien came to the shop and fell in love with Anna, later marrying her. The prince commissioned the portrait as a wedding gift to his bride.
Courtesy Beth Kimmerle Collection

But not every Baker's bar produces an off-putting bitterness when you bite into it. In 1852, Englishman Samuel German created a dark, sweet baking-chocolate bar while working for Baker's. It was named "Baker's German's Sweet Chocolate."

Over time, the apostrophe "s" in German's was dropped, giving rise to the urban legend that German Chocolate Cake is indeed from Germany. The first published recipe for this cake appeared in a Dallas newspaper, and came from a Texan homemaker. The name came from a key ingredient, the aforementioned Baker's product, and you can bet that General Foods, which owned Baker's by then, capitalized on the recipe's popularity.

Before fully assimilating into General Foods and eventually Kraft, Baker's sold a variety of chocolate-oriented goods: breakfast cocoa, German's Sweet Chocolate Bars, Caracas Vanilla Sweet Chocolate Bars, milk chocolate, chocolate tablets, and chocolate-flavored topping. When one considers the effect of larger corporations taking over the smaller, it is interesting to consider what was made of a product known as Walter Baker's Dessert, introduced in 1934.

A few years later it was given a name we all know — Jell-O Chocolate Pudding.

In keeping with his company's development of its chief product, Walter Baker released a book entitled *Cocoa and Chocolate*. The 1886 tome delves into the properties and various creative uses for Baker's Chocolate. At the time, Baker's offered the following products: Vanilla Chocolate, the ubiquitous German's Sweet Chocolate, Prepared Cocoa, Cracked Cocoa or Cocoa Nibs, Baker's Premium #1 Chocolate, Cocoa-Butter and Cocoa Shells, Caracas Liquor, Maracaibo Liquor, Eagle Pure Chocolate Liquor, and Cocoa Paste, to name a few. The last few items were intended for sale to confectioners for their own concoctions.

Today, Kraft sells Baker's products that are, "perfect for any baking occasion." Some are new like Baker's Dipping Chocolate, a microwavable chocolate treat intended as a dessert dip. But most have not changed much; the old-school Baker's Baking Squares, available in German's Semi-sweet, Unsweetened, Premium White Chocolate, and Bittersweet, still come in printed cardboard boxes with a modern version of our old-fashioned friend, "La Belle Chocolatière."

Vintage packaging. Sam German developed German's sweet chocolate for Baker's in 1852. In 1957, a Texas homemaker sent a recipe for chocolate cake — using German's chocolate — to a Dallas newspaper, leading to increased sales of the chocolate baking bars. Today, the overtly American cake is most often known as German Chocolate Cake, a sweet chocolate-buttermilk cake with coconut-pecan buttercream frosting.
Courtesy Beth Kimmerle Collection

Barry Callebaut

Swiss-based Barry Callebaut, which has two major processing plants in North America, is the umbrella company for a bevy of cocoa and chocolate-related products. In 1996, the 150-year-old Belgian chocolate producer Callebaut and the French manufacturer Cacao Barry joined forces to create a new chocolate company, Barry Callebaut. Individually, Cacao Barry and Callebaut boasted excellent reputations as makers of fine chocolate products, supplying confectioners and large manufacturers in the food industry.

Charles Callebaut started his business in Belgium as a malt brewery and dairy company in 1850. Initially, the company was involved in brewing, milling, and production of simple dairy products like butter and milk. That business grew from development of basic ingredients to manufacturing finished products. By 1911, Callebaut started production of chocolate bars and tablets for consumers, as well as the manufacturing of cakes and breads. The confectionary side of business grew, and by 1925, Callebaut was supplying its signature creamy couverture to chocolatiers. Soon the firm decided to concentrate exclusively on chocolate, and by the 1950s, the company was transporting liquid chocolate across Europe. In addition, Callebaut was gaining recognition as an export to the States. In 1981, Interfood, owners of Tobler-Suchard, took over Callebaut. Several mergers and transfers followed, and the company finally merged with Cacao Barry.

Charles Barry founded The Barry Group as a general food supply business in the United Kingdom in 1842. Cocoa was his top-selling product, and before long, Charles Barry started his own cocoa processing plant in Meulan, France. The Lacarré family bought out Barry in 1923 and expanded the business to include multiple chocolate plants. By the 1950s, Cocoa Barry had left the consumer products market and was concentrating solely on bean growing, roasting, and the making of chocolate. In 1985, they acquired Bensdorp Chocolate from the Netherlands, and eleven years later, Callebaut and Cacao Barry joined forces to create Barry Callebaut, adding van Houten and van Leer chocolate to the growing conglomerate.

In 2002, the combined Barry Callebaut acquired the German Stollwerck Group. Stollwerck is still headquartered in Cologne and manufactures chocolate products, including chocolate bars, packaged

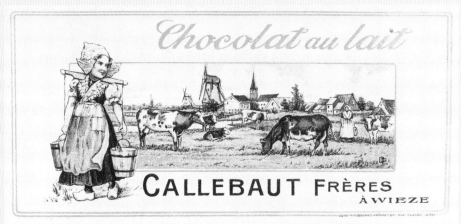

chocolates, and truffles. The company's confectionary tradition spans 150 years.

Started in 1839 by Franz Stollwerck, the firm initially produced medicinal cough drops. The business was a success and soon expanded its line to include other products. By 1860, Stollwerck was known throughout Germany for hard candy, chocolates, and marzipan. The Stollwerck Company became an international confectionary player and displayed a huge chocolate sculpture at the 1893 World's Columbian Exposition in Chicago. Its "Statue of Germania" exhibit was 38 feet high and sculpted on site from 30,000 pounds of chocolate.

By 1902, Stollwerck Chocolate owned and operated chocolate factories in London, Vienna, and Stamford, Connecticut. The Stamford factory was ranked as the second largest company in the entire United States, but the 1930s, with recessions and a looming war, were tough years for the company. After the war, Stollwerck faced a failing business and destroyed factories. Miraculously, the company rebuilt and reclaimed its title as the biggest chocolate maker in Germany. Under Barry

Callebaut, Stollwerck currently produces at a number of sites, primarily in Germany, and is known for its top-selling brand Sarotti, still the most popular chocolate in Germany.

In 1904, Emil J. Brach opened a small storefront in Chicago calling it "Brach's Palace of Sweets." The factory was in the rear of a building, and the selling area was in the front of the store. The Brach family built the business making and selling high-quality candies at a fair price. By 1939, Brach's was a leading manufacturer of fresh bulk candy and introduced its "pick-a-mix" concept in the 1950s, allowing consumers to mix their own bulk-wrapped candy. Brach's grew quickly into one of the largest U.S. candy companies, offering more than 500 varieties of candy. The Brach family sold the business in 1966 to American Home

Products. After several more ownership changes, Barry Callebaut acquired Brach's in 2003. Brach's continues to produce nearly 200 varieties of confections, including hard candies, caramels, and chocolates.

Today, Barry Callebaut is one of the largest cocoa producers and processors in the world; it comprises many well-known chocolate and confection companies such as Cacao Barry Van Leer, Callebaut, Van Houten, Luijckx, Bensdorp, Brach's, and Stollwerck Chocolate.

Vintage Images courtesy of Barry Callebaut

Blommer Chocolate Company

Started in Chicago, the hub of candy manufacturing, at the tail end of the Depression, Blommer Chocolate Company was the brainchild of the brothers Blommer: Henry Blommer, Sr., Al Blommer, and Bernard Blommer.

The Blommers weren't total strangers to the business; in fact, their father was one of the original partners in Milwaukee's Ambrosia Chocolate Company. Brother Henry brought experience; he had worked at the Ambrosia mill but decided that he'd rather do his own thing. With the aid of his brothers, they built a factory in the River West area of Chicago.

The brothers were hard workers, and in the early days of the business, they spent long nights at the factory, even setting up sleeping areas with cots and sacks of cocoa beans to watch operations closely. With the Depression barely over, economic times were still uncertain. But the tenacious brothers managed to squeeze out a profit in the very first year.

Blommer has since built two additional factories, in Los Angeles, California, and East Greenville, Pennsylvania. In 1952, Blommer bought Boldemann Chocolate of San Francisco and consolidated operations with the California factory in 1970, when they built a plant in Union City, California. Today, Blommer is one of the largest U.S. manufacturers of chocolate ingredients to confectionaries, specialty chocolate makers, and bakeries. It is one of only ten North American chocolate firms to oversee the entire chocolate manufacturing process — from the raw bean to the finished product.

Blommer's efficiencies and innovations in the early years have made the company one of the largest processors of cocoa in the United States; it annually grinds more than 100,000 metric tons at its three factories.

(Left) Bern Blommer, (Right) Al Blommer

Blommer's size and success made it an obvious target for a corporate takeover attempt in 1992. The large food processor Cargill moved in days after Henry, Sr. passed away, but the Blommer family, ever determined and hard working, fought the take over and convinced Cargill to back off.

Blommer is still a family-owned and family-operated business. Currently, Joseph Blommer runs the show; Henry Blommer, Jr. is the company chairman and CEO. Blommer's image is one of a company that "cares about its customers." The sales staff, customer service representatives, and technical personnel go the "proverbial 'extra mile' to make sure customers get help, support, and quality products." Such is the fate of a company who dedicates itself to the founding principles of quality, consistency, and concern for the customer.

As a supplier, the mainstay of Blommer business is with industry clientele. The individual consumer is not shut out, however. When in Chicago, you can visit the Blommer Chocolate Retail Outlet Store near the main factory on Kinsie Street. The outlet is very popular, selling the world's largest retail chocolate bar and hundreds of chocolate treats. There is also the Blommer Store Web site, which offers a bazillion Blommer chocolate products, the most exotic being Blommer cocoa shell mulch — a gardening product that is great for retaining water, forming vital nutrients, fighting weeds, and discouraging snails, slugs, and other garden pests. Plus, it smells like chocolate.

Henry Blommer

Founded by Henry Blommer Sr. and his brothers in 1939, Blommer Chocolate has grown into a leading North American processor of cacao beans. The brothers' father, William, had been in the chocolate business most of his life as one of the original partners in Milwaukee's Ambrosia Chocolate Company. They followed in their father's footsteps, first at Ambrosia and later in the establishment of Blommer in Chicago, Illinois.
Courtesy Blommer Chocolate Company

E.J. Brach Corp.

The son of German immigrants, Emil J. Brach traveled to Chicago in 1881 from his home state of Iowa. He began work in the office at the candy firm of Bunte Brothers & Spoehr, but he became tired of pushing paper and eventually moved to the position of salesman. Eager for independence and perhaps inspired by the profits that he witnessed, he started his own company. A resilient businessman, Brach blew $15,000 in an early candy-manufacturing venture that didn't pan out. Undeterred, Brach went into business in 1904 as a manufacturer and retailer of candy, opening a small shop at North and Towne in Chicago. Naturally, his wife and sons helped out around the shop named Brach's Palace of Sweets.

At first he sold caramels in the back of his store for the low cost of 20 cents a pound. Wanting more exposure, Emil sent his boy Frank by horse-drawn carriage to Siegel, Cooper & Co. and struck a deal to sell Brach's caramels at the department store.

That entrepreneurship and company success drove Brach's to relocate in 1906 to a bigger space on Des Plaines Street on Chicago's West Side. Several other stores, including Knox & Co. and Steele Five and Dime, began selling Brach's line of treats, which by then included peanut and hard candies.

A second move took place in 1909, this time to the corner of LaSalle and Illinois Ave. The next year, Brach's tenacious production output reached 2.5 million pounds, thanks in part to the addition of more hard candies and coconut nougats.

Upon relocating to a larger space at East Illinois Street in 1913, Brach's began hand-dipping chocolates, installed a marshmallow line, and added panned candies to his production.

By the beginning of World War I, Brach's had enlarged the East Illinois facility twice; he employed 200 candy makers and 250 salesmen; developed a clientele of 100,000 retailers throughout the nation; and was among the earliest businesses to make quality control part of the manufacturing process. For Brach's, this took the form of a state-of-the-art laboratory in which ingredients were tested to insure high standards were met.

Thanks to such incredible growth, Brach's was able to survive both the rationing of World War I and the

hardships of the Depression. By the end of the 1930s, Brach's was the nation's top maker of fresh bulk candy; sales had hit 90 million pounds and $9 million.

During the 1940s, Brach's concentrated on newer lines of candy products rather than the popular gift boxes and merchandising innovations of the 1930s. The company achieved great success with its candy bars featuring mint, coconut, pudding, and cherries. The Swing bar, named for swing music's popularity, was a top-seller. At one point it was the third-highest-selling, nationally distributed candy bar.

Distribution branched out into supermarkets, which had supplanted the old-time general stores of the previous era. Advertising expanded to include billboards, women's magazines, and radio shows. Holidays like Halloween and Valentine's Day became big candy events; the company promoted its candy corn and heart-shaped boxes in association with the popular dates.

Emil, who worked until his last days, died at age 88 in 1947. His sons had taken over in the 1940s and had raised the company's profile to reside among the largest candy companies in America. The boys focused on demographic appeal, as it were, concentrating on different segments of the consumer base and producing specifically for each group. When supermarket culture took off in the early 1950s, the brothers introduced the Candy Shop concept, a display cart from which one could buy candy year-round. This was a forerunner to the more familiar Pick-a-Mix display, introduced in 1958, from which customers mixed their own candy choices. Brach's ran night shifts to keep up with the demand. By the 1960s, Pick-a-Mix became so popular that the Chicago facility had to expand. Brach's produced more than 500 different candies in 1961 and began advertising on television, injecting their Pick-a-Mix carts into the national consciousness.

Edwin died in 1965, leaving Frank, by then 75, to run things. Due to his age and Brach's behemoth size, Frank sold the business to American Home Products in 1966. Arthur Bridges took over as president while Frank stayed on as chairman of the Brach's division.

American Home Products sold Brach's to the European candy and coffee enterprise Jacobs Suchard in 1987. Klaus J. Jacobs, principal stockholder of Jacobs Suchard, sold Jacobs Suchard to tobacco giant Philip Morris. He did, however, retain ownership of Brach's.

Jacobs became E. J. Brach's chairman of the board and bought all of Brock Candy Company's stock in 1994, merging with the Chattanooga candy outfit to become Brach & Brock Confections, Inc. The merger created the fourth largest candy company in the country and added a Gummi repertoire and growing fruit snack line to the company's domain.

As the company celebrates its centennial, Brach's Confections continues to grow under the wing of Barry Callebaut, which bought the company from Klaus Jacobs in September 2003. That same year, Brach's severed its Chicago roots to move most of its candy production to Mexico. The lower price of sugar has driven many companies south of the border.

Brach's still makes its Star Brite Peppermint, Milk Maid Caramels, and Maple Nut Goodies. In fact, Brach's currently makes more than 200 varieties of candies in all. Despite many changes in their first century of business, they are still known for their genius Pick-a-Mix concept.

Vintage images
Courtesy Michael Rosenberg Collection

92

Brach's Stars are pure goodness...
Brach's Finest _Real_ Chocolate
through and through! Next time
you're shopping, reach for the Stars!

©E. J. Brach & Sons,
Chicago, Ill.

Brach's Stars...
Finest _Real_ Chocolate!

All Brach's chocolates are
made with finest real chocolate.
You can taste the difference!

Brach's became famous for
its bulk candy concept, also
known as "Pick-a-Mix."
Customers filled Brach's-
branded paper bags with
caramels, starlight mints, or
non-pareils and bought
them by the pound. Today,
the company is owned by
Swiss-based Barry Callebaut
and produces much of its
classic bulk candy in Mexico.
Courtesy Michael Rosenberg
Collection

93

Brown & Haley, Inc.

Though Brown & Haley products are sinfully delicious, they do not constitute an unholy union. They met in church, after all, in Tacoma, Washington, in 1908. J. C. Haley had arrived from West Virginia in search of fortune, and he found spice, or at least a job, at Schilling and Company. Harry L. Brown already owned a small confectionery — selling, making, and experimenting with candy were among his passions. It's said that Haley complemented that passion with his marketing dexterity, though no one knows for sure how the idea to merge talents began. The two incorporated their candy-making business in 1914 under the name Brown & Haley.

Their efforts put Tacoma and their company on the map as a manufacturer of trademark, tasty treats. Though they had a full line of chocolate products, their first hit was the Mountain Bar. Originally called the Mt. Tacoma Bar and put on the market in 1915, the bar has a fondant vanilla center hand-dipped into a spoonful of tempered chocolate and ground peanuts. Today state-of-the-art machines make 592 a minute, but the bottom of the bar was originally smoothed off by hand. Left to solidify on a waxed card, it was then put in a blue, hand-folded box bearing a picture of Mount Tacoma, now called Mount Rainier. In 1923,

the name was changed to Mountain Bar. That same year, the boys hit really big with what would become their signature delight, Almond Roca. This is one candy rock known 'round the world. In an event even more preciously innocent than meeting in church, Brown & Haley let the concoction be named by a librarian who thought Roca (rock in Spanish) suited the candy's brown, irregularly shaped toffee center. Brown developed the recipe, which consists of butter-crunch toffee surrounded by chocolate, rolled in diced almonds, and wrapped in gold foil. Since then, more than five billion Almond Roca nuggets have been sold, and its deliciousness is recognized worldwide, due in part to its groundbreaking packaging.

In 1927, the duo sought a longer shelf life for its fresh-made product. Almond Roca was the first candy to be packaged in a sealed tin — a pink one, at that. The innovative packaging reflected Haley's marketing genius, as it kept candy fresh, was easy to transport, and was instantly recognizable with its unique color. During World War II thousands of stay-fresh tins were sent to troops overseas.

News of the delectable candy spread like wildfire to achieve international fame. Sir Edmund Hillary took it to the top of the many Himalayan mountains he

scaled; Brown & Haley were considered "Confectioners to the Court of the Emperor of Japan," where the rock is still considered a delicacy; and Beverly Sills, Shirley McLaine, and Rosie O'Donnell are a few modern celebrities who swear by it. Currently sold in sixty-three countries, the "candy that travels" is clearly one of America's favorite confections.

The company has expanded five times since 1919, a testament to the success of the Almond Roca and Mountain Bar as well as to sound management. The company, though, is a considerable small fish, ranked eighty among *Candy Industry* magazine's list of 100 top candy companies.

Incidentally, Fred Haley, who ran the company until 1984, was and is something of a legendary character. An early social activist, he attended Martin Luther King, Jr.'s "I have a dream" speech and made many enemies with his progressive thinking. He was anti-apartheid and refused to join the chamber of commerce because it wouldn't stop doing business with South Africa; he refused to fire an employee who stood up for himself, invoking the Fifth, during the McCarthy era; he fought for minority rights and desegregation (and suffered boycotts in doing so); and he opposed Japanese-American internment during World War II. Fred has been honored many times, not only for his controversial past but also for his continuing support of social causes. Tacoma

Employees did much of the chocolate finishing processes by hand in the early years.
(Left) Candy centers troop through a chocolate enrober.
(Bottom right) Workers pack and weigh tins of Almond Roca.
(Bottom left) Chocolate pieces are packed to be shipped to stores.
Images courtesy Brown and Haley

ALMOND ROCA
REG. U.S PAT OFF. COPYRIGHT 1944
America's Finest Confection
MADE FROM FRESH CHURNED BUTTER,
MILK CHOCOLATE, SUGAR, ALMONDS,
COCOANUT OIL, SALT, VANILLA
FLAVOR, LECITHIN

designated him as a Tacoma Hometown Hero, the State Legislature adopted a resolution honoring his public service in 2000, and the University of Washington, Seattle, and the Business Examiner Group gave him a lifetime achievement award.

There have been three generations of Haley's at the helm, and the company recently elected Anne E. Haley, granddaughter of founder J. C. Haley, to serve as Chairman of the Board. Pierson Clair is now president & CEO, after having served several years as president and COO. Combining their fresh talents, Anne and Pierson have set the controls for tasty.

Today, 92 years later, Almond Roca is recognized around the world as the delicious, unique buttercrunch toffee drenched in chocolate and wrapped in gold foil and pink packaging. Consumers will also delight in new Cashew Roca, wrapped in a bright blue foil.

Brown & Haley's product line started with chocolate treats, and from the beginning, Mr. Brown sought ways to produce an American chocolate that could rival European delicacies in taste and price. The company continues the innovation and confection excellence started by J. C. Haley and Harry Brown.

Cadbury Schweppe's, Ltd.

For many in the United States, the name Cadbury conjures up one thing only — its famous chocolate Creme Eggs. But the Easter treat hardly represents the world's second largest company and its full line of products, rich business and social history, and standing in the contemporary chocolate market.

The progenitor of the ten children, Richard Tapper Cadbury was born in Exeter, England, in 1768. He started a drapery and fabric business in Birmingham six years shy of the millennia, and in time became a distinguished citizen. Already the Cadbury name was synonymous with public service, progressive thinking, and social consciousness.

His son John, the actual founder of the Cadbury chocolate business, was born in 1802. At sixteen, he became an apprentice to a tea dealer. Six years later, when his tutelage ended, he returned to Birmingham and began selling tea, coffee, and drinking chocolate on his own. Cocoa and chocolate drinking had been a staple among England's elite since the 1650s.

Cadbury actually ground his own cocoa using a mortar and pestle. He imported the beans from South and Central America and the West Indies and created a range of cocoas and chocolate drinks mixes; his customers bought the product in blocks, flaked off a quantity, and added hot water or milk to create the finished cocoa drink. Although expensive, the cocoas and drinking chocolates were quite popular, and his business began to flourish. He made a name for himself by advertising his healthy and delicious tonics.

By 1831, John dropped teas and coffee from his offerings and concentrated wholly on chocolate and drinking products. He began a full-time manufacturing venture located in an old malt house and had sixteen types of drinking chocolates and eleven cocoas by 1842. These were not your average Ovaltine but were made with ground cocoa, added nutrients, and starchy ingredients that absorbed the excess cocoa butter. As a devout Quaker, Cadbury firmly believed in the health benefits of drinking chocolate over liquor; he listed these nourishing concoctions under names such as Churchman's Chocolate, Pearl and Homeopathic Cocoas, and the mysterious sounding Iceland Moss Cocoa. In 1847, Cadbury expanded again by renting a larger factory in the center of Birmingham, and taking the name Cadbury Brothers of Birmingham. By then, John's brother Benjamin had joined him in manufacturing the brown gold.

In the mid-1850s, taxes on cocoa beans were lowered, giving a broader customer base to the industry. This also boosted competition. The 1850s were hard times for Cadbury brothers, despite receiving its first Royal Warrant in 1854 as manufacturers of cocoa and chocolate to Queen Victoria. The partnership between John and Ben dissolved in 1860, and John retired a year later, leaving the business to his sons Richard and George. John Cadbury died in 1889, having lived out his final years as a dedicated civic and social activist.

With the lean years of the family business behind them, Richard and George sought ways to improve their products, mainly the taste. Taking a page out of Dutch manufacturer Van Houten's book, they purchased a Van Houten press, with which they could produce pure cocoa butter and cocoa powder. Their new chocolate mixes no longer needed potato flour, sago flour, or the other starchy ingredients that, according to George Cadbury, made their original cocoa taste like a "comforting gruel." The new, purer product was christened Cocoa Essence and advertised as "Absolutely Pure . . .Therefore Best" and represented a turning point in the company's history. It became immensely popular, with the help of heavy advertising and endorsements from the medical and trade communities. From this time forward, the Cadbury Company traveled the path toward establishing an empire with a brisk yet respectable trot.

Cadbury introduced the chocolate box, filled with high-quality chocolates. Decorated with pictures and designs created and painted by Richard himself, Cadbury became the first company to put idyllic images — fluffy kittens, frolicking children, and lush landscapes — on its chocolate boxes, rather than simple printed labels. This began an industry trend toward fancy boxes and innovative, collectible chocolate packaging, with Cadbury's boxes a fast favorite in Victorian England.

Fry's produced dissolvable chocolate tablets for drinking in the late 1700s, and by the late 1800s, it had produced one of the first chocolate eating bars. Cadbury merged with Fry's in 1919.
Courtesy Beth Kimmerle Collection

A milestone in the company's history occurred in 1878, when the brothers purchased 14.5 acres of countryside about four miles south of Birmingham and established a "Factory in a Garden." Believing the squalor of industrial city life to be detrimental to just about everything (including birth rate, education, and personal fulfillment), they named this site Bournville. The brothers had keen Quaker interests in nature, housing, and social rights and sought to create a village community to accommodate both employees and nonemployees. Housing, schools, religious spaces, exercise facilities and fields, massive gardens, and other fixtures of a socially progressive experiment were built in time as the brothers' Bournville grew in both size and ambition. Just as the social benefits of this plan began to flower, the business side developed as well, eventually becoming self-sufficient in the chocolate-making process. The Bournville Village Trust was established by George to preserve the living experiment and protect its natural environment from speculators. A charitable trust devoted to the extension of the Bournville estate and the promotion of housing reform is still overseen by Cadbury descendents, who remain active in social reform to this day.

Richard, the great marketer of candy who created the first heart-shaped Valentine's Day candy box, died in 1899. George became chairman of the new board of Cadbury Brothers, Limited. Also named to serve on the board were his two sons, Edward and George, Jr., and Richard's sons, William and Barrow.

By 1897, milk chocolate had become a target for research and development, given the success the Swiss were having by producing it their way. Cadbury's initial experiments and outcomes did not match the Swiss milk chocolate in taste or quality. Though they cribbed the Swiss use of condensed milk, Cadbury's introduction of a superior milk chocolate bar did not occur until 1905. That year marked the introduction of Cadbury's eventual bestseller, Cadbury's Dairy Milk. Today, annual sales of the milk chocolate are upwards of 250 million bars.

In 1908, Bourn chocolate, "the original dark chocolate," was introduced and, five years later, the company built another factory in Gloucestershire. With the start of World War I, Cadbury's altruistic stripe once again showed itself as the company sent books, clothes, and, of course, chocolate, to the front lines. The company also set aside funds and accommodations for returning veterans and the survivors of the dead.

The war years also saw the culmination of a partnership with J. S. Fry & Sons, a company with its own deep and rich history in chocolate. In 1729, the progenitor, Walter Churchman, was presented a Letters Patent by George II for "the sole use of an Engine by him invented for the expeditious, fine and clean making of chocolate to greater perfection than any other method in use . . . ." A Bristol apothecary, Churchman pursued the substance for its supposed medicinal qualities. He and his peers, however, came to realize that with a little tweaking, the healthy mixtures could also serve as delicious beverages. In 1761, after the death of Churchman's son Charles, Dr. Joseph Fry took over the business, its patent, and Churchman's recipes. No stranger to the mystical arts of chocolate making, Fry developed his own techniques and recipes, eventually producing a sweetened chocolate tablet that would dissolve in hot milk or water; he called it Fry's Bristol Chocolate.

His son, Joseph Storrs Fry, took over after his father's death in 1787, and the business, considered the oldest chocolate firm in England, became J. S. Fry & Sons.

Fry's company pursued innovation, quality, and expansion vigorously and introduced its own edible chocolate in 1848. By 1902, Fry introduced a milk chocolate bar known as Five Boys Chocolate, a popular treat until it was discontinued in 1976.

Fry's snazzy treats became icons in their own right, and many are still winners for Cadbury: Fry's Turkish Delight, flavored with Otto of Roses and covered with milk chocolate; Crunchie, a "crisp, close honeycomb texture covered with deep layers of milk chocolate;" Fry's Chocolate Cream; and lastly the Curly Wurly, the celebrated cousin of the defunct old Mars favorite, the Marathon Bar.

Although famous, robust, and sporting a vast product line and many awards, Royal Warrants, medals, and diplomas, Fry's was taken over by Cadbury in 1916; in 1919, the two officially merged, becoming the British Cocoa and Chocolate Company. Finally, in 1935, Fry became a wholly owned subsidiary of Cadbury Group, Limited. In 1923, the year of George Cadbury's death, Cadbury built a factory to accommodate Fry's manufacturing in Somerdale, where it still operates today.

The success of the Cadbury's Dairy Milk led to the introduction of the Cadbury Milk Tray in 1915. Chocolates were put onto trays in special five-and-a-half-pound boxes and sold loose to customers. In 1916, the assortment was packaged in a half-pound fancy box, and a full pounder followed in 1924. The spin was that these boxes represented a good, no-frills buy for the common man. They still are one of the more popular assortments in England today.

In the years to come, Cadbury introduced products that remain great sellers and capture the palates of the country: Cadbury's Flake; Cadbury Creme Eggs (but the egg as we know it did not get laid until 1971); Cadbury Dairy Milk with Fruit and Nut; Bournvita, a "healthy tonic of malt, milk, cocoa and eggs;" Cadbury's Buttons; Mini-eggs, solid, candy-coated milk chocolate egg-shaped candies; and Wispa in 1983.

Much of the Cadbury process shares the high-tech style with any number of James Bond villains. That is to say, much of the chocolate-making process is automated, highly sophisticated, top-secret, and computer-controlled. The company buys its beans from Ghana and Malaysia and roasts and processes them at the Cadbury cocoa factory located in Chirk, North Wales. As is common to all manufacturers dealing with the entire chocolate-making process, Cadbury puts the chocolate through its paces of conching, tempering, adding ingredients, molding, and packaging. The difference with Cadbury is, of course, the recipes that the company uses, the ingredients, and the variety of tempering techniques set one type of chocolate treat apart from the others. By using specifically designed, highly developed equipment, factories such as the Creme Egg Plant in Bournville can produce 70,000 eggs an hour, 50 million chocolate pieces a day, 598 chocolate bars a minute, and 1,800 tons of chocolate a week.

You can purchase a Cadbury product in most stores, though some brands are not easily found in America. In England, you could jaunt over to a Cadbury Cocoa House and experience "café culture," replete with all the chocolate treats you could want. Or perhaps you'd visit Cadbury World, four miles south of Birmingham. There, visitors can witness chocolate-making demonstrations, appraise fresh liquid chocolate, and participate in enrobing. Though it's not a factory tour, it offers a look at the packaging plant, possibly in operation.

In 1969, Cadbury merged with Schweppes to become Cadbury Schweppes, one the largest international companies in the world, selling candy and beverages in more than 200 countries, employing 55,000, and making many favorite products, from Dr. Pepper to Sour Patch Kids. Although Cadbury Schweppes might be rather intimidating in size and scope, the socially progressive beliefs and actions begun by ye olde Cadbury's Chocolate still have a prominent place in its organization, and the chocolate-inspired tradition lives on.

DRINK BETTER CHOCOLATE

Here is a new kind of drinking chocolate — Cadbury's 'Cup' Chocolate. When occasion demands it can be prepared *in an instant.* Simply by shaking the soft flakes straight into a cup of boiling hot milk.

CADBURY'S 'CUP' CHOCOLATE

REDUCED PRICES

Cadbury Schweppes is one of the biggest beverage and confectionery companies in the world. With a history stretching back over 200 years, its products — from Dentyne to Dr. Pepper — are available around the world.
Courtesy New York Public Library

Elmer's Candy Corp.

In 1845, 16-year-old German Christopher Henry Miller arrived in New Orleans, where he had come to seek his fortune. He got a job at a pastry shop, assisting the baker, and spent time learning English when he wasn't cooking. At 24, the ambitious Miller finally realized his immigrant dream and gained U.S. citizenship. Shortly after, he married Mary Wetzel, and opened the Miller Candy Company on the corner of Jackson and Levee streets. Miller was soon well known for his integrity in conducting business and for being a man of high standards. He was also noted for his delicious chocolate confections and handmade pralines.

When he died in February 1902, one of his eleven daughters married a man whom Miller greatly respected, Augustus Elmer. Elmer and three of his brothers-in-law then changed the name of the thriving confection business to Miller-Elmer's. By 1914, when Augustus's sons joined the business, the name was changed to Elmer Candy Company to reflect what they were known for throughout the region. For the next sixty years, the business expanded and flourished in several factories, producing different types of confections, preserves, and snacks sold throughout the United States. In the early 1960s, in an effort to continue the expansion of the business, the family added a partner to the company. In 1963, Roy Nelson purchased the entire company from the Elmer family, and moved the plant to Ponchatoula, 45 miles from New Orleans, to make a bigger and better factory.

By the 1970s, the company found itself competing with many other companies producing the same products, and it decided to focus on one specialty, seasonal boxed chocolates. Although this meant the loss of some old regional favorites, business flourished when Elmer concentrated on what the company had made since the beginning: fine chocolate.

Elmer's is currently the second largest heart-box chocolate manufacturer in the United States. Elmer's continues to produce quality chocolates and will soon be run by the fourth generation of the Nelson family.

Elmer's has been a New Orleans favorite for years. Today, it concentrates on producing heart-shaped boxed chocolates for Valentine's Day.
Courtesy Elmer's Candy

Ghirardelli Chocolate Company

One of the oldest continuously operating companies in America, Ghirardelli Chocolate Company is among the ten American chocolate companies that engage in the complete chocolate manufacturing process — from the bean to the bar.

The founder, Domenico (later changed to Domingo) Ghiradelli, is an interesting chocolatiering entrepreneur, with a background rife with intrigue. Hailing from Rapallo, Italy, he was the son of a noted Genovese chocolatier and learned the trade from him. In 1837, Domingo and his first wife sailed for Uruguay, where he took a job in the chocolate and coffee trade. He then traveled to Lima, Peru, in 1838 and set up his own confectionery shop. It was while in Lima that he became friends with James Lick, a proprietor of cabinets. Lick decided to move to San Francisco, following the rumors of gold and taking 600 pounds of Ghirardelli's chocolate with him. In 1848, soon after Lick's arrival, the gold rush began and Lick sent word that the chocolate was a hit. Domingo's wife died, and he pulled up stakes to try his hand in the search for treasure.

Ghiradelli settled near Jamestown-Sonora in 1849, his heart set on striking it rich. When the prospects of doing so turned grim, he quit prospecting and opened a general store to hock his chocolate and other provisions to the hopeful miners. After several years, Domingo relocated to San Francisco and incorporated in 1852 under the name Ghirardelli & Ghirard. As his business flourished, his Italian family arrived stateside, and he was inspired to change the company name to Mrs. Ghirardelli & Co., to honor his new wife.

Legend states that an employee in 1865, for reasons unclear, hung a bag of cacao beans in a warm room and noticed the cocoa butter separating and dripping out, leaving a residue that could be processed into ground chocolate. Dubbed the Broma Process, the technique of separating cocoa butter from beans is still used in the industry today.

By 1884, business was booming: the company had 30 employees and exports of Ghirardelli's products (which included wines, cordials, and liquors — soon dropped in favor of chocolate, coffee, and spices) traveled throughout the United States to the far east and Mexico. Ghirardelli's sons became partners in the family business, and the company moved its manufacturing base to the Pioneer Woolen Mill, on the Northern Waterfront in San Francisco, in 1893. Through the years, this space was enlarged and developed to accommodate growth; it became a vast corporate complex before it was fashionable. A power house was built in 1915 to meet energy needs; an apartment building was constructed to address the housing needs of employees; and a beautiful clock tower, designed in the style of Chateau Blois in France, was erected. In 1923, two new stories topped the Cocoa Building and the famous Ghirardelli sign was added on top. (Pearl Harbor fever in 1942 darkened the sign for defense reasons.) By 1964, the historical waterfront area was known by the name Ghirardelli Square and was declared a city landmark a year later.

In addition to bringing Old World chocolate to America, Domingo Ghirardelli also showed ambition in advertising, nearly blanketing the west — and eventually the country — with billboards, posters, unique packaging, etc.

One particular Ghirardelli chocolate favorite, no longer

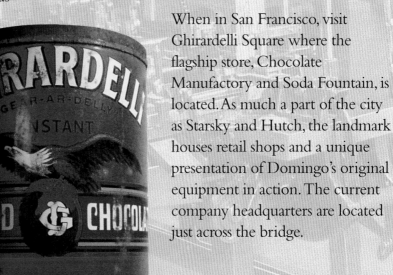

1930s Ghirardelli's cocoa can.
(Background) Workers feeding finished chocolate cakes into a wrapping machine, 1926.
Courtesy Beth Kimmerle Collection

made, was called Flicks. Though immensely popular, the packaging machine, made before World War I, was severely damaged when the headquarters relocated to San Leandro. Tragically, the machine could not be repaired, and a Flick hysteria mounted as production ceased. The chocolate bits are still fondly remembered.

In 1998, the Swiss Chocolate company Lindt and Sprungli acquired Ghirardelli, remaining a wholly owned subsidiary of their holding company. Ghirardelli is one of the few and proud chocolate companies in America to take the bean to the bar, and it continues to produce baking and beverage products — chips, bars, and cocoa powder — spanning the chocolate spectrum from white to unsweetened dark.

When in San Francisco, visit Ghirardelli Square where the flagship store, Chocolate Manufactory and Soda Fountain, is located. As much a part of the city as Starsky and Hutch, the landmark houses retail shops and a unique presentation of Domingo's original equipment in action. The current company headquarters are located just across the bridge.

Wrapping Cake Chocolate

Guittard Chocolate Company

Rather than finding gold on a journey to the Barbary Coast in early 1860, 22-year-old Frenchmen Etienne Guittard found that the best way to thrive as a gold digger was to fall back on his skills as a trained chocolatier. At first, he traded his uncle's fine French chocolate for necessary mining supplies. He set out for the hills, but the imported chocolate's popularity among miners led the Frenchman to return to Paris and raise the money necessary to start a company. San Francisco was an ideal marketplace, with a harbor for importing beans, newly rich patrons, and other French and Italian confectioners who had brought their sweet skills stateside. Etienne returned to the city in 1868 and opened Guittard Chocolate on Sansome Street. It was a successful entry into the confectionery game from the very start.

Etienne handed the business down to his son, Horace A. Guittard, who distinguished himself by rebuilding an improved plant in the Embarcadero on Commercial Street after the massive 1906 Earthquake and fire. Amidst the devastation, Horace created opportunity, while many businesses shut down or closed entirely. He expanded the company by selling a line of coffee, tea, and spices along with the classic

Guittard Chocolate line. Then his son Horace A. Guittard took over in 1950 and oversaw the move into mass production and automation. Lead by Horace A., the company sold its Embarcadero factory to the city of San Francisco, and the main facility was relocated to Burlingame, California, in 1955. The new plant was at the top of the industry in terms of modernity; there was even a street named after it in the newly developed area of Burlingame. The company was small, working to please the tastes of individual clients, and also a behemoth of the wholesale chocolate industry, serving big names in the ice cream, pastry, and confectionery industries. West coast See's Candies was — and still is — their largest client. Under Horace's stewardship, the truffle trend also started to flourish, and the gourmet chocolate chip was introduced to the refined cookie-makers of the world. These epicurean advancements continue to positively impact Guittard's high-quality manufacturing.

Horace's son, Gary, is the current president and CEO and the fourth generation Guittard candy maker. Having spent his childhood in the world of chocolate, Gary has built-in chocolate instincts. His new contribution of gourmet, artisan chocolate is elevating the candy to the status of fine wine.

Gary is responsible for creating the E. Guittard line,

named to honor the company's founder. The line was implemented to pay homage to the company's past and uses a combination of old and modern equipment, methods, and recipes in its production. E. Guittard, sealed with a vintage Guittard illustration, supplies the burgeoning artisan foods market. The signature beans have different flavor profiles, derived much from where they are grown, and their tastes are described in the lingo befitting a wine-tasting (notes of fruit, a light acidity). New blends have been concocted such as the L'Harmonie blend, a dark chocolate with sixty-four percent cacao, and Soleil d'Or, a thirty-eight percent milk chocolate. The line continues to grow, offering everything from snack-size bars to 2.2-pound bars intended for pastry chefs and small confectioners.

Guittard Chocolate imports the finest beans from the most exotic locales — Java, Ghana, Venezuela, Trinidad, Ecuador, Columbia, Brazil, Madagascar, and New Guinea — for all of its products. Flavor profiles and cultivation conditions determine overall selection; the Criollos of Venezuela or Java, the Forastero of Ghana, and the Trinitario from Trinidad are some examples of the quality beans shipped directly to the company's headquarters and 75,000 square-foot plant in Burlingame. Each blend of bean is tested and then roasted separately to induce and preserve its unique flavor; winnowing and stone grinding follow; and additional ingredients like sugar and vanilla are added to create the final refined flavors.

Guittard is well known by many pastry chefs for their top-quality chocolate. They now produce premium eating bars named for Etienne Guittard, the company founder.
Courtesy Guittard Chocolate

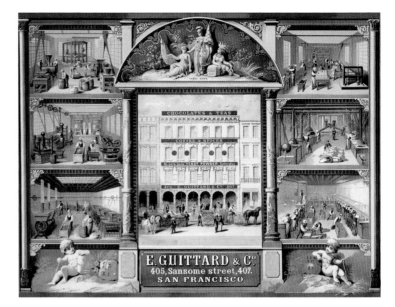

Both a retail and wholesale operation, Guittard's has made its mark on the industry by offering time-tested and family-honed "special" recipe chocolate. Whether it's a bag of Guittard's Smooth 'N Melty Mints or a wholesale ten-pound bar, it is a welcome part of the classic Guittard experience.

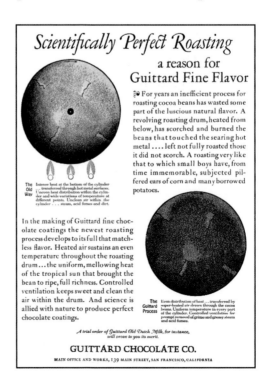

Hershey Foods Corp.

When discussing the subject of chocolate, Milton Hershey, the man who became the Henry Ford of American chocolate, must be mentioned. With his know-how, vision, and tenacity, he turned a small industry into a successful dynasty. Milton Hershey's Milk Chocolate is an American tradition.

Some refer to his start in chocolate as the dawn of the decline of pure chocolate; many before him produced inferior product filled with strange, inedible, nonchocolate matter. Hershey's successful formula cannot be ignored, however. He succeeded in making consistent chocolate in an efficient, cost effective fashion, introducing millions to a tasty product that previously was exclusive, expensive, and sometimes lacking in quality. Like it or not, Milton created an icon.

Milton Hershey was a Mennonite from the small Pennsylvania village of Derry Church. By the time he was eighteen years old, he had opened his own candy store in Philadelphia. However, the marginally successful shop failed after six years, and Milton moved to Denver, Colorado, where he learned how to make mass-produced caramels using fresh milk. In 1886, Milton moved back to Pennsylvania and started his lucrative Lancaster Caramel Company. In 1893, Hershey, now a successful candy maker, attended the World's Columbian Exposition in Chicago. He was impressed by German chocolate machinery and purchased some for his caramel business. At the Chicago show, Boston confectioner, Lowney's, exhibited chocolate bars that might have also caught his attention. Attending the show was a business turning point for Milton. A year later he formed the Hershey Chocolate Company and produced Hershey chocolate caramels, breakfast cocoa, and baking chocolate.

At age 42, Hershey sold his Lancaster Caramel Company for a tidy one million dollars. At the time, this amount was enough to live on happily ever after. But Milton was driven by a dream and not just dough. His newly formed chocolate division was separate from the caramel business sale. He kept his chocolate-manufacturing equipment along with future rights to manufacture chocolate products. He believed that a market existed for affordable confections that could be produced on a large scale. His hunch would prove correct.

He returned to his birthplace of Derry Church, Pennsylvania, and started his chocolate-manufacturing operation. It was located in the heart of dairy country, where the fresh milk needed to make milk chocolate was available. His plant also was located near the ports of New York and Philadelphia, plus he could draw upon the hard-working people of the area for his employee base. By 1903, he began to build what is now one of the world's largest chocolate manufacturing plants. It officially opened in 1905 and introduced mass produced chocolate with the first bars that rolled off its production line.

Hershey's chocolate business and the community he established flourished. His blossoming chocolate village soon contained a school, park, churches, golf courses, and a zoo. He set up his town to provide workers with easy access to the factory and activities to entertain and educate. The first product to join Hershey's Milk chocolate bars was Hershey's Kisses, added in 1907. (Each chocolate drop was originally hand-wrapped in a square of silver foil, and machine automation included the signature paper plume by 1921. The plume branded it genuine Hershey's chocolate.) By 1911, four years after Derry Church changed its name to Hershey, chocolate sales had reached an astonishing five million dollars per year.

In addition to his business vision, Hershey was a great philanthropist. Unable to have his own children, he started a school for disadvantaged youth called the Hershey Industrial School in 1909. In March 1915, Hershey's dear wife, Kitty, who had been terminally ill, died. After her death, Hershey donated his entire estate to the Hershey Trust for the benefit of the school. His estate included thousands of acres of land and all his stock in his successful chocolate company. Today, the Milton Hershey School is the largest residential grade school in the United States. The school provides free education (pre-K through 12), housing, clothing, health care, and counseling to thousands of children, representing a number of diversities, who are in financial and social need. Hershey put his fortune to good use; the school benefits from his original gift, which is now worth more than five billion dollars.

Hershey Foods Corporation is the largest North American manufacturer of both chocolate and confectionary products, with revenues of over $4 billion and more than 13,000 employees worldwide. The Hershey Chocolate Company owns many famous Hershey chocolate candies and brands including Almond Joy and Mounds candy bars, Hershey's Milk Chocolate, Hershey's Kisses, Bubble Yum Gum, Kit Kat, Reese's Peanut Butter Cups, Jolly Rancher, Twizzlers candy, Whoppers, and York Peppermint Patties.

Milton Hershey's strong convictions about charity, community, and chocolate have made him and his chocolate an American legacy.

In 1898, Hershey developed a symbol for its trademark. As Milton began to concentrate on producing chocolate, he created an image of a small child enjoying chocolate while riding in a cacao pod. It appeared on cans of cocoa until 1936, when it was replaced by the block lettering so familiar today. Courtesy Beth Kimmerle Collection

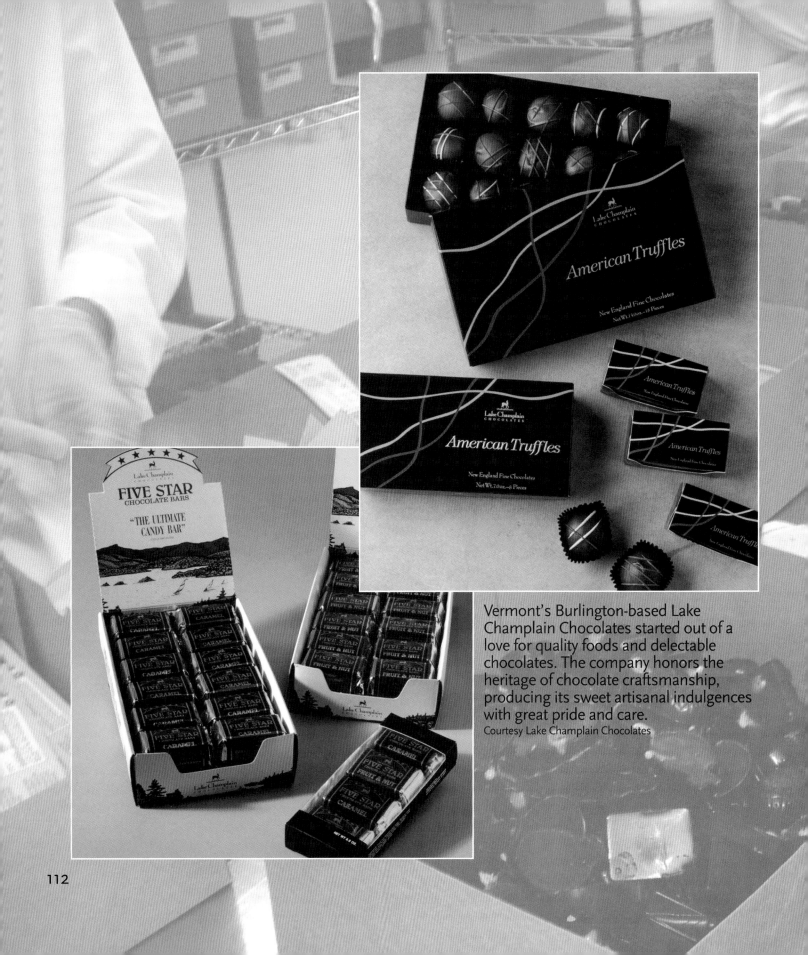

Vermont's Burlington-based Lake Champlain Chocolates started out of a love for quality foods and delectable chocolates. The company honors the heritage of chocolate craftsmanship, producing its sweet artisanal indulgences with great pride and care.
Courtesy Lake Champlain Chocolates

Lake Champlain Chocolates

Jim Lampman was a true epicure early in life. At age fourteen, he was working at neighborhood restaurants, and a few years later, he was whipping up chocolate fudge in front of fascinated onlookers. Jim's love of food drew him to pursue its art and science in both life and work. In fact, he became the first male student in more than 100 years to major in home economics when he attended the University of Vermont, graduating in 1972.

By 1983, Lampman owned a celebrated Burlington, Vermont, eatery. The Ice House Restaurant served gourmet food and became known for unusual treats. Lampman's experimenting chef, dissatisfied with the chocolates his boss was known for giving his staff, surprised him with his own version of chocolate truffles. Lampman enjoyed the delectable chocolates so much that he began serving them to his customers. The hand-rolled, deliciously flavored truffles were soon in great demand, and Lampman founded a boutique chocolate company to supply the growing business. He eventually sold his restaurant to concentrate on the sweet life.

Lake Champlain Chocolates started with classic truffles and expanded its repertoire to include amazing candy bars. In 1989, Lampman's Five Star Bars were named "Best New Bar" by Ray Broekel in the candy connoisseur monthly, *Candy Bar Gazebo*.

Burlington, Vermont, remains the headquarters and production site of Lake Champlain Chocolates. No longer a small storefront operation, the company makes delicious chocolate bars, unique truffles, hot chocolate mix, and boxed chocolates for customers across the country. The creation and product of a true foodie, Lake Champlain Chocolates are still made with fresh, natural ingredients and are still simply delectable.

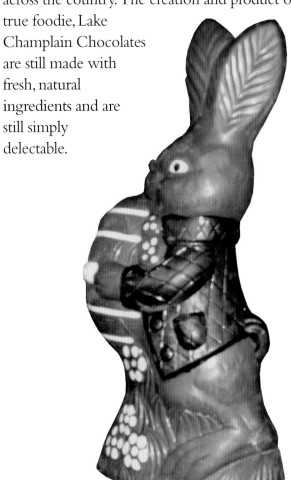

Madelaine Chocolate Novelties

Jack Gold and Henry Kaye were enterprising brothers-in-law who started a simple business, making boxed chocolates in a warehouse in downtown Manhattan. Both were Holocaust survivors who had come to the United States to work for their cousins at Barton's Candy. They quickly learned the confectionary business and founded their own firm called Madelaine Chocolates in 1949.

The inspiration for the company name came from an elegant 1940s movie starlet who, to the two men, was the epitome of class and sophistication. They were eager to make fine chocolates suitable for someone glamorous like her and honored the company with her name. By 1954, the partners had expanded the business and were concentrating mostly on foil-wrapped chocolates that, until then, were an imported European luxury item. From the beginning, the chocolate company ordered its foils from Italy and its molds from Germany, maintaining that such details were as important as the quality of the chocolates enclosed.

As the business expanded, it first moved to Brooklyn and then to Rockaway Beach, New York, where the growing headquarters and production facilities are still located.

Madelaine's niche remains molded chocolate. The company purchases pallets of huge chocolate blocks and tanker trucks of liquid chocolate for molding its foiled chocolates. Once injected into the appropriate mold via a molding machine, the chocolate is flash frozen and refrigerated. Some molds undergo further refinement or, in the case of hollow chocolate molds, are spun in order to create an empty center. From this point, the smaller candies are foiled, wrapped, and boxed automatically, while larger, more ornate creations are hand-wrapped.

Before long, the second generation of family members were running the business, including Jack's granddaughter, and her husband, Jorge. Today, they are running a company with more than 500 employees and a massive manufacturing facility that covers three city blocks. Madelaine Chocolates, still producing finest quality foil-wrapped eggs, coins, and rabbits, are sold in stores throughout the United States.

Madelaine Chocolates is famous for its delicious molded and foiled chocolate shapes, ranging from cigars to cars.
Courtesy
Madelaine Chocolates

Mars, Inc.

M&M's, Snickers, and Three Musketeers are customary chocolate candies, seemingly on display at every deli, drugstore, and supermarket on the planet. They hold a reserved space in the choicest spots in all vending machines; they are never far from reach.

But long before Mars owned top-selling brands of confections, it was a small chocolate company operating out of a modest American home.

Frank Mars and his wife, Ethel, started their company in Tacoma, Washington, in 1911. They made and sold a variety of chocolate-dipped buttercream candies from their home kitchen.

It is said that in 1920, after a visit to a drugstore with his son Forrest, Frank Mars thought that chocolate malted milk might be a fine flavor idea for a candy bar. Soon he devised a portable candy bar, made to taste like a malted milk drink that could be enjoyed anywhere. The Milky Way Bar was appealing because it comprised an airy nougat center covered in chocolate. With its fluffy inside and far-out name, it looked bigger than other plain chocolate bars on the market. It was one of the first combination candy bars, made from a variety of ingredients, and it appeared at the beginning of America's candy bar craze. The Milky Way Bar was an immediate success. Soon, Mars built a large factory in the suburbs of Chicago to service the entire country and produce other popular favorites, including Snickers and Three Musketeers. Frank Mars was laying the foundation of what would become a global snack food business.

In the 1930s, Frank's son Forrest introduced the Milky Way to England but called it Mars Bar. Along with candy, Forrest grew his Euro-based business by making and selling pet food and instant rice. His biggest contribution to Mars may have been to give chocolate a protective candy coat to prevent it from melting. Forrest was said to have discovered shell-coated chocolate pieces while visiting Spain.

Bruce Murray, a business partner who had worked for Hershey Chocolate, developed the chocolate formula for Forrest's idea. The pair honored the colorful chocolate candies with their last initials, naming them M&M's. The easy-to-eat, bite-size candies were soon adopted as a favorite of U.S. forces during World War II. The chocolate bits were packaged in cardboard tubes and gained appreciation as a convenient snack that traveled well in any climate. In 1948, their tubular packaging was changed to the paper pouch we know today. (Mars still uses tubular packaging in its special holiday issues at Easter and Christmas.) Then in the mid-1950s, their famous slogan, "The milk chocolate melts in your mouth — not in your hand," debuted on television. Today, in their vast array of colors, M&M's chocolate pieces are celebrated the world over.

Always a leader in innovative chocolate production, Mars, Inc. is busy researching the health benefits of cocoa by studying the nutritional effects of chocolate. They now market a flavanol-rich chocolate.
Courtesy Mars, Inc.

Leo Stefanos developed the chocolate-coated ice cream Dove Bar for his two young sons. They always darted after the neighborhood ice cream truck whenever they heard the sound of its musical jingle approaching. To keep them safe from oncoming traffic, he spent months developing his own ice cream treat.

The Stefanos Dove Bar became the talk of the Chicago neighborhood. By the late 1970s, Leo's son Mike took over the successful small ice cream business. The popularity of the delicious chocolate-dipped ice cream continued, and the beloved Dove Bar brand was acquired by M&M Mars in 1985. Introduced nationally in 1990, Dove Dark Chocolate is now Mars's upscale premium chocolate brand, consistently winning taste tests around the globe.

By the 1970s, Mars, Incorporated, still family-owned, was a global conglomerate, making everything from chocolates to pet food and vending machines to radios. Privately held, Mars claims to have grown from a $300 million business at the start of the 1970s into a $14 billion business today.

Mars brands — 3 Musketeers, M&M's, Skittles, Milky Way, Snickers, Starburst, and Twix — continue to appear on top-selling candy lists. And Mars, Inc., still family owned, churns out Uncle Ben's Rice and pet food like Whiskas. While Mars chocolate brands are certainly ubiquitous, the site of a few brightly colored M&M's rolling about an open palm is something no one has ever complained about.

Vintage images courtesy Mars, Inc.

Nestlé

Henri Nestlé was born in Frankfurt, Germany, in 1814, and moved to Vevey, Switzerland, while in his twenties. First a merchant, druggist, and small-scale inventor, he became interested in food manufacturing and experimented with various recipes for baby food to help mothers who were unable to breastfeed.

Nestlé eventually came up with a cooked milk formula he called farine lactée, that was based on, in his words, "wholesome Swiss milk and a cereal component baked by a special process of my invention." In 1867, he fed his mix to a premature baby boy whose mother was dangerously ill; the boy lived, and Nestlé's reputation grew. Nestlé condensed-milk production followed, and he opened an office in London to handle the new business. Within five years, he was exporting his baby formula around the globe. By 1874, he sold his company for a million francs, and the company, still bearing the Nestlé name, started to diversify. In 1929, Nestlé bought out chocolate makers Peter, Cailler and Kohler, a European company specializing in chocolate for chefs and bakers. Its founder, Daniel Peter, pioneered the world's first milk chocolate, using Henri Nestlé's condensed milk recipe to make the groundbreaking concoction.

Nestlé was a global company by 1938, the year it introduced the Nestlé Crunch candy bar, a consistent top seller today. Hershey introduced its rice and milk chocolate Krackle Bar the same year. Toll House morsels were also launched in 1938 and remain an American baking tradition. The baking chips were formulated for a popular chocolate chip cookie recipe invented by a New Bedford, Massachusetts, innkeeper for her Toll House restaurant. Several years later, World War II inspired the launch of Nestlé's newest product, Nescafé, which became a staple of the U.S. military.

Nestlé Quik chocolate powder was introduced in 1948 and quickly rose to the best-selling chocolate flavoring for milk in the United States, with popular television advertising featuring Farfel the dog, a singing puppet, who exclaims: "N-E-S-T-L-E-S, Nestlé's makes the very best . . . chocolate."

NESTLÉ

E TRÉSOR DES MAMANS

By the mid-1960s, Nestlé was Switzerland's biggest company, a huge multinational firm, incorporating more than 200 factories around the world, with global management still based in Henri Nestlé's adopted town of Vevey.

In the 1980s, Nestlé acquired the popular candy brands Chunky, Bit-O-Honey, Raisinettes, Oh Henry!, Goobers, and Sno-Caps from Ward-Johnson. Goobers and Sno-Caps are movie-house favorites, and Oh Henry! remains a classic American candy bar, made with caramel, peanuts, and fudge.

The Williamson Company of Chicago introduced Oh Henry! in 1920. Some say it was named after the famous ball player Hank Aaron, but the true story goes much differently. George Williamson owned a candy shop visited often by a young customer whose name was Henry. The young girls who

In 1930, Kenneth and Ruth Wakefield bought a Cape Cod-style house in Massachusetts. Constructed in 1709, the house originally served as a rest stop for road-weary travelers. The Wakefield's opened their house as a lodge, calling it the Toll House Inn. Ruth's homemade meals and desserts soon attracted visitors from all over New England. Once, while making cookies, Ruth cut a bar of semi-sweet chocolate into tiny bits and added them to her dough, expecting them to melt. Instead, the chocolate pieces softened to a creamy texture. The resulting cookie became immensely popular, and the recipe was soon published on the wrapper of Nestlé's Semi-Sweet Chocolate Bar. By 1939, the bits were offered as the ready-to-use morsel drops we still know today.
Courtesy Beth Kimmerle Collection

worked there enjoyed his visits and started asking favors of him, clamoring, "Oh, Henry, will you do this?" and "Oh, Henry, will you help with that?" The requests became a regular occurrence, and Williamson decided to dedicate a new candy to the popular lad.

Nestlé continued to add to its historic chocolate family, and by 1990, it had acquired Curtiss Brands, maker of Baby Ruth and Butterfinger candy bars, officially making it a monster candy company of world favorites. In the 1920s, Baby Ruth was the world's most popular candy, with sales of more than five million bars a day. In 1937, Admiral Byrd's expedition to the South Pole carried thousands of Baby Ruth bars. Throughout the last century, Baby Ruth has been a popular part of America's candy history.

Today, having swallowed up confectioners and chocolate companies alike, Nestlé employs almost a quarter of a million people, produces everything from pasta to pet food, and purchases more than 10 percent of the world's crops of coffee and cacao beans.

Peter's Chocolate

Daniel Peter had a taste for business and market trends. A butcher's son, he worked in a grocery owned by a Madame Clement, who produced handmade candles to sell in her store. She turned over the candle-making operation to Peter, who, as a budding entrepreneur, soon realized that the use of wax candles was fading and kerosene was taking over the market.

His girlfriend's father, Francois-Louis Callier, was a master chocolatier, as were Callier's sons. Once Peter married Fanny Callier, the winds of change had completely blown out the candle business, and he looked for opportunity in chocolate. Some believe that Peter traveled from Vevey to Lyon, France, and apprenticed himself to a chocolatier. What is known is that he was immersed with chocolate-making heavies and learned the business quickly.

In 1867, Peter returned to Vevey and set up shop as a chocolate maker, converting Madame Clement's candle-making facility to a chocolate factory. His new operation was successful, and he began to lay the foundations for Peter's Chocolate. As an in-law to the prestigious chocolate-making Callier family, he was heavily influenced by their work and techniques. By some accounts, he followed his brother-in-law, Auguste Callier, into the business. His father-in-law, after all, had established Switzerland's first chocolate factory in 1819. Also, in the time between 1867 and 1875, it's certain he met with Charles Amadée Kohler, developer of a popular hazelnut chocolate. Kohler started out as a merchant but moved on to making chocolate in 1830. Like many other chocolatiers, Kohler and Peter experimented with their original products — out of curiosity or to stay ahead of the competition — and it led to Kohler's hazelnut chocolate and to Peter's Chocolates.

Peter eventually etched his name in the chocolate bar of history in 1875 at age 31. It was then that he perfected a recipe for milk chocolate. His first success was considered decent if it was eaten before the milk spoiled. The key to his long-term success was the input from Henri Nestlé, a local baby food maker. Nestlé sought a way to give milk to the infant son of a friend, as the baby was allergic to breast milk. Nestlé was able to successfully withdraw the water content from the milk, creating a sterile condensed milk. Peter's initial chocolate bars used this same milk heating method before adding cocoa to the mix. But he truly perfected his chocolate when he used Nestlé's condensed milk in his recipe.

Peter's delicious and long-lasting product made him the champion of the chocolate world. Some debate surrounds the name of his booming new company, with Peter's Chocolate Company as one version and Peter-Kohler Chocolate Company as the other. Peter acquired Kohler's business and his factory, and, ultimately, the Callier family name was added to create the Peter-Callier-Kohler Swiss Chocolate Company. For thirty years, they produced milk chocolate using Nestlé's condensed-milk recipe.

Peter's company eventually became the world's largest supplier of milk chocolate, and the same formula Peter developed is still used today.

Young Daniel Peter's company didn't completely go wholesale. As the popularity of his milk chocolate spread so did his standing in the culinary circles of Europe. He exhibited his innovative products at expositions, winning many awards for his creations, and became a fine marketer and salesman.

In 1901, a representative from the American firm Lamont, Corlis and Company happened upon Peter's Gala Bar in England. The man convinced his superiors of the chocolate's potential profitability, and the American firm secured the rights to sells Peter's products in North America. By 1906, Peter's company opened a plant in Fulton, New York. It was located next to a Nestlé factory that had been built a few years before in Upper New York State's cow country. His European factories were maximized with their homeland's demand and could no longer import comfortably to American shores. The Fulton factory started producing milk chocolate the next year, and Peter bought the neighboring Nestlé factory in 1909.

The winding road to Nestlé's buy-out of Peter's company in 1929 is a murky one. Some suggest that the Callier Chocolate Company merged with the Swiss General Chocolate Company and this is how the company named the Peter-Callier-Kohler Chocolate Company came into being in 1911. The word from the Peter's is that the American distributor Lamont & Co. bought Peter's at some point before Nestlé. Nestlé was a distributor of Peter's products, too, and, while the details following are unclear, it is certain that Nestlé and Peter's walked a chocolate era together. Like true milk chocolate, the stories pleasantly mix together to create a secret recipe for historians.

After Nestlé bought Peter's company, chocolate began to dominate Nestlé's diverse line of products as a consequence. Nestlé introduced its own extensive line of consumer bars and Peter's became its industry wholesale line. But Nestlé's major focus was on consumer products, and in 2002, Wilbur Chocolate, a subsidiary of Cargill, Inc., bought Peter's from Nestlé. At the time of the sale, Wilbur maintained that Peter's long-standing brand would continue. With Wilbur and Peter's recognized brands, Cargill added to their growing list of chocolate and food ingredients.

Headquartered in Lititz, Pennsylvania, under Wilbur's base of operations, Peter's sells wholesale confectionary goods to baking, dairy, ice cream, and candy making industries throughout North America. The backbone of all Peter's products remains special recipes, whether it's in chips, chunks, caramels, cocoas, coatings, or inclusions, and the unifying aspect of Peter's wide variety is its chocolate and the spirit of innovation that lead to its development.

In 1875, Daniel Peter was the first to make a truly marketable milk chocolate bar. By 1908, his Swiss Peter's Chocolate Company was making its milk chocolate at a plant in Fulton, New York. Eventually, Lamont, Corliss, and Company purchased Peter's Chocolate Company, which became Nestlé's Chocolate Company in 1951. In 2002, Peter's Chocolate was purchased by Cargill, Inc.
Courtesy Michael Rosenberg Collection

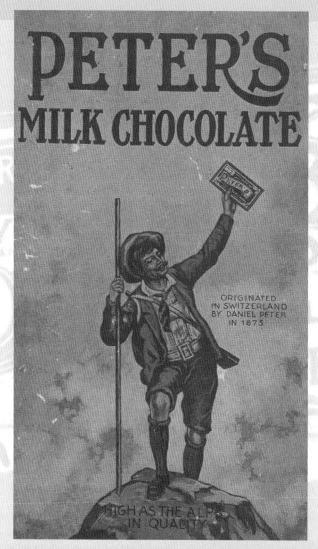

HALF A CENTURY AGO with his little Swiss oven, Daniel Peter could make only a few pounds of milk chocolate a day.

TODAY, in the Peter's American factories alone, several thousand pounds are made every hour.

The same fine original blend of fifty years ago

HALF a century ago in the tiny Swiss village of Vevey, the neighbors of Daniel Peter used to laugh at him for "fussing around day and night in his kitchen." But Peter was too absorbed to notice or care. He was intent on one idea.

And at last he won out. Peter not only originated milk chocolate—one of the most perfect food-confections ever worked out—but he perfected the *Peter's* blend.

In those days, with his little Swiss oven, he could make only a few pounds a day. Today, in the Peter's American factories alone, several thousand pounds are made every hour. But the *Peter's* blend has never been changed.

Today *Peter's* is the same fine blend perfected by Daniel Peter—the blend that has remained the standard of quality for two generations.

Of the scores of varieties of cocoa beans but six go into *Peter's*, and only certain choice grades of these. It is an art—roasting and blending these beans. Much of the flavor depends upon this process.

And the *Peter's* process is still a secret. In our big American factory only foremen thoroughly trained in Swiss methods have charge of this work.

Peter's is different—distinctive. It's *good*. You'll like the fine, rare flavor of it.

Ask for *Peter's* today.

HIGH AS THE ALPS IN QUALITY

If unable to obtain Peter's promptly, write to Lamont, Corliss & Company, 131 Hudson Street, New York, sole selling agents.

Plain · Almond Bars & Croquettes

125

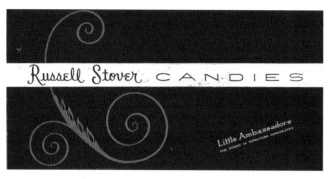

Russell Stover Candies

Early on, Russell Stover took steps toward starting what eventually would become a candy empire. The road was a long one, filled with detours, rest stops, and missed turns. Before marrying the woman who would figure prominently in the Russell Stover company history, Stover was working for the American Tobacco Company in Chicago. Before that, he was studying pharmaceutical arts at the University of Iowa.

On June 17, 1911, Stover married Clara Lewis and was bequeathed farmland in Saskatchewan Province, Canada. A year later, he gave up the farming life, and for the next nine years, he bounced around Canada and the United States with his wife in tow. On two separate occasions during those scattershot years, the two had tried to start their own candy business and failed.

His fortunes changed in 1921 when, as the head of candy operations for the Graham Ice Cream Company, he met Chris Nelson, the inventor of the chocolate-covered Eskimo Pie — the first popular ice cream bar. The two became partners in marketing the product.

The Eskimo Pie was a wild success, with sales topping $6 million for the next two years. However, Stover sold his share in the venture for a mere $30,000 in 1923, as most of the money made from the pies was lost to litigation fees; the Pie was illegally copied many times over.

That same year, the Stovers moved to Denver and successfully started another candy company. From their bungalow, they made and marketed Mrs. Stover's Bungalow Candies; one year of "home-fashioned" chocolate sales enabled them to open five stores in the Denver area. From there, they expanded into Kansas City and St. Louis, Missouri, and Lincoln and Omaha, Nebraska. By 1931, the company decided to move its headquarters to Kansas City, Missouri, barely surviving the Depression and World War II. The company's name was changed to Russell Stover Candies in 1943.

For the next three decades, Stover was family-run, and had established a regional empire with its hand-dipped chocolates and boxed candies. By 1931, it was one of the largest boxed-chocolate manufacturers in America, neck-to-neck with Whitman. Russell died in 1954, a millionaire and member of the Chocolate Hall of Fame; Clara, who sold Stover four years after Russell's demise, died in 1975. An author, she wrote and published *The Life of Russell Stover — An American Success Story* in 1957.

In 1960, Louis Ward bought the company and went on to transform its regional candy business into an international empire. At the time of its sale, Stover had about thirty-five of its own stores and two thousand retailers selling its chocolates. By purchasing other companies (such as Whitman's in 1993 and Pangburn's Chocolate Company in 1999), aggressively expanding and advertising, and developing a broad, mid-to-low-priced product line, Ward — and later his sons Thomas and Scott, the current heads — achieved sales in all fifty states, Canada, and Puerto Rico. They had factories in Cookeville, Tennessee, Montrose, Colorado, Corsicana, Texas, and Abilene and Iola, Kansas; distribution centers in California, Colorado, Texas, Kansas, Indiana, Virginia, Florida, and New Hampshire; employees estimated at about six thousand; fifty Russell Stover stores, and some forty thousand wholesale accounts at drugstores, groceries, department stores, and the like throughout North America. In the words of Louis Ward, "We became famous because we made great pieces of chocolates that you didn't have to take out a mortgage to buy."

Now the largest seller of boxed chocolates, Russell Stover maintains its promise that every piece made is hand-dipped — over 25 million a year. A confectionery, it buys only the finest ingredients from other suppliers, including its chocolate. Individual pieces are prepared in small batches, following the instruction of Mrs. Stover's 80-year-old recipes. Interestingly, after experimenting with a variety of more efficient techniques over the years, the Wards have always come back to Mrs. Stover's recipes; her cooking equipment, like copper pots and Hobart mixers to blend ingredients; and her methods, including slower cooling of the cremes, and, of course, hand-dipping.

Stover's boxes still sport the trademark Stover ribbon from the early days when boxes were hand packed and tied with a fancy ribbon. Stover also continues to produce a mecca of treats, whether milk chocolate or dark chocolate, creams, caramels, toffees, nuts, or coconuts.

Beginning with the tasty Eskimo Pie, Russell Stover was a chocolate pioneer. On July 13, 1921, Christian K. Nelson and Stover made an agreement to market and produce America's first chocolate covered ice cream bar. The name was changed from Nelson's "I-Scream Bar" to "Eskimo Pie." Nelson and Stover sold Eskimo, and Stover quickly started another chocolate business. By the 1930s, the Russell Stover Chocolate company was one of the largest boxed chocolate makers in the United States.
Courtesy Beth Kimmerle Collection

127

Scharffen Berger Chocolates

Located in Berkeley, California, Scharffen Berger Chocolates is the newest American chocolate processor to join the list of companies that import fermented cacao beans and turn them into captivating chocolate. Friends Robert Steinberg and John Scharffenberger, sharing a passion for quality chocolate and living life well, started the company in 1996.

Steinberg, a family physician, had stopped his full-time practice in 1990 due to incurable lymphoma. His love of food and science lead him to an internship at Bernachon Chocolatier in Lyons, France. In the traditional European methods, he learned the craft of chocolate.

Scharffenberger had just sold his successful boutique wine cellar, Scharffenberger Cellars, to LMVH Moët Hennessy-Louis Vuitton when Robert approached him with the idea of making artisanal European-style chocolate. Their combined backgrounds and experiences seemed ideal.

Scharffenberger's skill in creating a successful food business fit naturally with Steinberg's recent European confection tutelage. In 1996, the two friends experimented with different cocoa beans in Robert's kitchen, using primitive methods: pestle and mortar, hairdryer, and coffee grinder. The next year,

with imported, vintage chocolate-making equipment, they made their first chocolate batch in a South San Francisco factory. Further experiments and a passion for perfection led to a delicious-tasting chocolate.

The new Scharffenberger factory is located in Berkeley, where the company produces small batches of pure dark chocolate and conducts factory tours. They also have a visitor-friendly store in San Francisco's Ferry Building.

Using vintage machinery, Scharffen Berger makes its fine chocolates with an emphasis on tradition and artistry.
Courtesy Scharffen Berger Chocolates

See's Candy 1960's Pasadena Rose Bowl Parade Float.
Courtesy Beth Kimmerle Collection

See's Candies, Inc.

When Charles See left Canada in 1921 to try his hand at the confection business, he decided that no image would better reflect the personality of his fledgling venture than that of his mother. Apart from using her recipes as a foundation, Charles See knew that keeping things in the family was the only way to bring about the kind of lovingly crafted product he desired.

See, along with his mother, Mary, and his wife, Florence, opened the first See's Candies shop and kitchen on Western Avenue in Los Angeles in November 1921. The sparkling clean, black and white shop was designed to resemble Mary See's home kitchen.

Benefiting from the wide acceptance of an unusually high-quality candy, See's was able to grow steadily from that first shop to twelve shops by the mid-1920s and thirty shops during the Depression. By 1936, See's was able to expand to San Francisco.

Mary See died in 1939 at the age of 85, but the company's ability to adjust to changing times — without abandoning the passion for quality and service that Mary See represented — kept it going strong throughout the decades to come. Following World War II, See's Candies grew as California grew, opening up shops throughout the state. In the 1950s, See's established itself with the new and growing phenomenon of shopping malls. Customers valued the See's Candies product for its quality and taste and continued to visit See's old-fashioned black and white shops, enjoying their trip to a time past where service was paramount.

In 1972, the See family sold its company to Berkshire Hathaway, Inc., presided over by Chairman Warren Buffett. Utilizing his philosophy of acquiring solid companies where he could follow his hands-off policy, Buffett installed Charles N. Huggins as President and CEO.

See's Candies are sold in more than two hundred shops throughout the West, and the company maintains the family atmosphere Charles See established, with many employees working there for several decades. Mother Mary See, spectacled and silver-haired, still smiles with pride from candy boxes shipped throughout the world. Her old-fashioned virtues of homemade quality and friendly service turned out to be the best ingredients in her original chocolate recipes, savored by millions to this day.

Thompson Candy Co.

In 1871, at age seventeen, Thompson Candy's founder, William H. Thompson, left his East Haven, Connecticut, home to discover life. The road soon lead to making chocolate in Philadelphia, a hotbed of the confectionary arts, where Thompson became an apprentice to Steven F. Whitman, founder of Whitman's Chocolate, and began his career as an aspiring chocolatier.

After nearly a decade as an employee at various Philadelphia confectioners, Thompson set himself up as a specialty manufacturer of confectionery in the up-and-coming town of Meriden, Connecticut. Among his first offerings were cream walnuts, bon bons, caramels, chocolates, frozen pudding, and ice cream.

In 1895, Thompson transformed his modest two-story storefront. He and his wife lived in the apartment upstairs; below was a full-fledged ice cream parlor and confectionery. Five years later, he moved the business to a larger building with a staff of sixteen employees. Candy was produced in the back, ice cream in the basement. Chocolate cigars and other molded treats were on the menu, as were the popular candies of the day: licorice, candy corn, pralines, and nonpareils. Though the lavish parlor and catering service that Thompson established were profitable, Thompson's ambition drove him to keep pace with the industrial revolution and large-scale candy manufacturing. By the late teens, he had built his own chocolate factory.

Besides being a shrewd businessman, Thompson had a reputation as one of the first to use milk chocolate in his chocolate-molded products. With a staff of forty, he manufactured bon bons filled with fruits, nuts, and almonds and vast armies of chocolate soldiers, eagles, bunnies, Santas, fish, frogs, lobsters, chickens, hearts — anything a holiday, celebration, or sense of whimsy desired. His bon bons were hand-dipped and molding was also done by hand, usually by women. Thompson's products sold well in his own store and soon lined the shelves of drugstores and other retailers from Maine to the nation's capital.

By June 25, 1929, Thompson's company had become incorporated as the W. H. Thompson Co.; it left retail permanently and focused strictly on manufacturing for others. The business thrived during the flapper era, and Thompson established himself as one of the

Northeast's top candy men. But on June 26 of the same year, he was dead of a massive heart attack.

His son Charles E. Thompson took over the company and, in September 1934, staged a going-out-of-business sale. The repeal of Prohibition, the Depression, and other problems of the day had taken their toll on the company. But rather than give up completely, Thompson, who had worked every job in the factory under his father's tutelage before taking over, registered the name Thompson Candy Co. and simply downsized the operation.

One obstacle to a full rebound was World War II; interestingly, Thompson turned over his plant to the production of war materials, a decision owing much to the shortage of raw materials at the time. By 1951, Chuck's son George reluctantly took over the company with the goal of focusing on molded specialties and simply selling out. During this period, Thompson moved into automation, eventually mass-producing wholesale molded eggs and Santas for large retail customers such as Russell Stover and See's.

In 1967, George sold the company to Yale-educated engineer Knowlton White. With an eye on profit and longevity, White brought on the likes of Marshall Field's as customers. He also updated and expanded his manufacturing capabilities and, like William Thompson had done before him, he indoctrinated his sons into the chocolate-molding arts. White died and left the business to his sons, Jeff and Allan, in 1978.

In the early 1900s, Thompson Confectioner supplied ice cream, candies, and ices around New Haven, Connecticut, from a horse-drawn carriage.
Courtesy Thompson Candy Company

Improving upon their father's dedication to the Thompson brand and his ambition for growth, the boys continued to pursue new equipment, larger production space, and more customers by stepping up advertising and visits to trade shows. This strategy paid off and revenues increased greatly in the first five years of their tenure.

Thompson's niche remains molded chocolate, and the company remains headquartered in Meriden, Connecticut. Thompson is primarily a private-label chocolate novelty company, most famous for its chocolate cigars, coins, and molds befitting practically every occasion.

Whitman's Chocolates

To many, the words Pennsylvania and chocolate conjure up Hershey and usually only Hershey. But before Milton was even a chocolate sprinkle in his father's eye, a Quaker by the name of Stephen F. Whitman had already formed his own confectionary company on the streets of Philadelphia.

Whitman's Candies traces its roots to 1842, when Whitman, nineteen years old, set up a "confectionery and fruiterer shoppe" on Market Street, close to the waterfront. It's quite possible that, upon tasting various European imported treats, Whitman decided there was something to be had by making his own locally. Subsequently, he purchased loads of imported fruits, nuts, cocoa, and flavorings necessary to produce a line of candies highly comparable to the pricey but popular European confections of the day. He did what many American entrepreneurs would do if they saw a demand for something expensive — he made his own, cheaper.

According to several sources, Whitman's shop sold a mix of various European imports and his own individual chocolate pieces. He introduced his own box of chocolates in 1854, the Whitman's Choice Mixed Sugar Plums, a precursor to the world-famous Whitman's Sampler. Whitman's keen marketing sense was responsible for much of his success; the sugarplums were packaged in an "elegant box, pink and gilt, lavishly decorated with designs of rosebuds and curlicues." Whitman Candies also advertised heavily in the Philadelphia business directory, area newspapers, and magazines. His savvy business approach was responsible for the spread of his candies throughout the Northeast and as far west as Chicago.

In 1866, Whitman expanded into a second building and began offering a wholesale line of bulk candies intended for sales under the names of its purchasers. In 1876, he was awarded a bronze medal for excellence at the Philadelphia Centennial Celebration, and by 1877, Whitman's Candies began selling Instantaneous Chocolate — the first of many tin-boxed products to come. International fame reached Whitman's in 1878, when his chocolate products were highly reviewed at the Paris Exposition.

Predictably, Stephen's son Horace, an apprentice confectioner, took over in 1888. Horace revolutionized the packaging industry by introducing cellophane to the process. He saw it used in Europe as a decorative packaging material. He brought samples home, believing the clear, thin film could be used to keep the contents of his boxes fresh. He also thought the cellophane added a clean look and was eye-catching. When DuPont began making cellophane in 1924, Whitman's was their biggest customer.

In 1906, Whitman's moved again to a bigger facility. A long-enduring advertising venture began three years later when product ads started running in *The Saturday Evening Post*. The company was incorporated as Stephen F. Whitman & Son, with Horace as president, that same year. With his father's business sense coursing through him, Horace began distributing directly to dealers. Whitman's awarded its franchises to the classier drugstores, promising distribution to only one drugstore per town and thereby ensuring loyalty with their exclusive offer. Walter P. Sharp took over the company in 1911 and put a "money-back guarantee" into effect, a highly advanced tactic for its time. He also introduced the still-sold Fussy Package for Fastidious Folks.

The Whitman's Sampler introduced a guide to filled chocolates on its box lid and became the best-selling chocolate box in the United States as a result.
Courtesy Beth Kimmerle Collection

But Sharp's sharpest move, one that would keep the Whitman name on the tongue of anyone without a chocolate allergy, was the creation, production, and marketing of the Whitman's Sampler. Sharp had a needlework sampler on his wall, and its design and linen background caught his eye. He began an almost Holy Grail quest to arrive at the right "feel" for a sampler to represent Whitman's. A woman, known around town for her skill with a needle, worked from artist's sketches to produce a sampler that suited Sharp's vision. Her sampler was reproduced then lithographed and used as the cover paper of a hinged candy box filled with Whitman's bestsellers. The product came with an index that showed which candy corresponded to its position in the box, a brilliant innovation itself, iand by 1915, the Sampler was the best-selling candy box in the United States. To acknowledge this, Whitman's created the Messenger Boy, a trademarked symbol and candy piece.

The Sampler had many styles and themes. Partnering with what eventually became the Book of the Month Club, Whitman's created the Library Package — small, pocket editions of classic literature combined with a pound of select chocolate pieces. This Sampler was changed into Service Chocolates — Sweets with a Book — during World War I, designated as a gift for overseas servicemen. The 1920s saw the creation of some fancy art-oriented boxes, including the Lebrun Box, fashioned for Mother's Day and based on a painting by French artist Marie Anne Elisabeth Vigée-Lebrun. For World War II, Whitman's created the Land, Sea & Air tins, a chocolate survival kit fashioned after a sardine can.

In the 1920s, Whitman's expanded its chocolate line to include fountain syrups, sauces, and icings, and Louis L. McIlhenney took the reins from Sharp. The Depression saw sales plummet, but a stubborn Whitman's, refusing to sacrifice quality, opted instead to increase its advertising to remind people about the pleasures of chocolate.

The Sampler experienced some significant changes in the years before World War II. Compartments, insets, and the "pillow puff" liner were added; the colors were brightened in 1941; and the box received the French Edge treatment — the top and bottom edges extended past the sides. The company's memorable slogan, "A woman never forgets a man who remembers," was also conceived during these years. After World War II, the Whitman's Sampler box began to resemble its current packaging.

Postwar years introduced another innovation, the refrigerated display case. This thunderbolt kept chocolate cool and fresh during the summer months and was developed in partnership with General Electric. By 1950, close to 10,000 of these open-top refrigerated displays were sold and installed; some dealers reported sales increases of 300 to 600 percent. Legend has it that McIlhenney actually came up with the idea a decade before while experimenting with a pane of glass inserted into an icebox door.

New technologies and keen business sense continued the candy company's success. In the 1950s, Whitman's recognized a world where fame is currency and began using celebrities to endorse its products. Popular movie stars like Bob Hope and Elizabeth Taylor appeared on chocolate boxes and in advertising. Whitman's also made the jump to television, becoming one of the first chocolate companies to air commercials. In 1961, the company moved again, this time just outside of Philadelphia. A 37-acre campus was established, complete with a factory covering ten of those acres. New products were developed and marketed, beginning in 1977, to keep pace with America's changing tastes and culture: chocolate bars, chips, baking chocolate, hard candy sticks, Danish butter cookies, and an expanded holiday line. In 1984, Whitman's introduced Light Chocolate with one-third less calories than normal products. The company's place in American history was cemented in 1991 when the Smithsonian Institution introduced the Sampler and other company artifacts into displays at the National Museum of American History.

In May 1993, Whitman's Candies was purchased by Russell Stover's Candies and still remains a privately held affiliate. Stover's, a Kansas City–based empire, moved Whitman's operations to Missouri — a very controversial and litigation-ridden decision. Philadelphia was sad to see one of its oldest companies go; it was bitter, not bittersweet. The Eastern factory fell quiet for the first time in decades, used only as a warehouse for imported cacao beans.

The Whitman name is a hot commodity for Stover's because of the Whitman's Sampler. Indeed, the Sampler icon is the key to Whitman's survival. It's still the highest-selling box of chocolates, especially around Valentine's Day, when they sell around four million. Stover's has determined that, year-round, a Whitman's Sampler is sold every 1.5 seconds. Under Stover's roof, Whitman's produces a wide variety of boxed arrangements. Given the popularity and economy of this favorite, whether for a holiday or for the heck of it, the Whitman name, now an American icon, will no doubt persevere.

Wilbur Chocolate Co.

Henry Oscar Wilbur ran a hardware business in Vineland, New Jersey, and in 1865, Wilbur saw that, by partnering with Philadelphia confectioner Sam Croft, the grass could be greener on the candy side. The two formed Croft & Wilbur and set up shop at 125 North Third Street, Philadelphia, producing mainly molasses and hard candies. These candies found their most enthusiastic customer was the railroad, which would in turn have "train boys" peddle them to eager passengers.

After incorporating chocolate-making into their repertoire, the entrepreneurs found that they needed additional space to keep up with the demand for their confections; they built a facility at 1226 Market Street. Still growing in 1884, they established the company of H. O. Wilbur & Sons as a result of the decision to separate cocoa- and chocolate-manufacturing from the rest of the business. Croft and a new business partner, Mr. Allen, made candy under the moniker Croft & Allen, while Wilbur focused on chocolate; three years later, H. O. Wilbur & Sons moved into larger quarters at the intersection of New and Bread Streets. Still successful, Howard retired and left the work to his sons, William Nelson and Harry L. Wilbur.

Howard was still inspired by chocolate, and in the 1890s, he came up with the enduring Wilbur Bud. Introduced in 1893, these dollops of chocolate took their name from their resemblance to a flower bud, the result of an experiment in primitive, yet fanciful molding by Howard. The Wilbur Buds were made from "Velour," or specially formulated, sweet dark chocolate, that was deposited in small amounts into intricate, flower-patterned molds.

When Lawrence H. Wilbur, third-generation chocolatier, joined the company, he used his tutoring in Germany's chocolate arts to invent a machine that wrapped the Wilbur Buds in foil. In 1909, the company was incorporated under the name H. O. Wilbur & Sons, and another facility was built in Lititz, Pennsylvania, in 1913.

As extensive as the Wilbur family tree is, it hardly holds a candle to the list of merged and purged companies that eventually came to rest under the

Wilbur name. Nearby in Lititz was the Kendig Chocolate Company, which was originally founded as a caramel company in 1900. Two years later, Kendig was bought out and renamed Ideal Cocoa and Chocolate Company; the new plant was built in Lititz. Ideal was famous for its chocolate cigars, Nut Lunch Bars, Ideal Almond Bars, Noah's Ark Chocolates, and Ideal Brand Cocoa. In 1927, Ideal merged with Brewster Chocolate Company of Newark, New Jersey, to become Brewster-Ideal Chocolate Company.

Meanwhile, at H. O. Wilbur & Sons, heavy negotiating was taking place between the Wilburs and the Suchard Société Anonyme of Switzerland. To get a foothold in the United States, Suchard wanted its chocolate manufactured and sold by Wilbur, and in 1928, the two merged to form the Wilbur-Suchard Chocolate Company. Soon after, they merged with the Brewster-Ideal Chocolate Company and created a chocolate vortex that remains strong in Pennsylvania Amish country today.

Once the dust from the merger had settled, the company had a factory in Newark, Lititz, and Philadelphia,

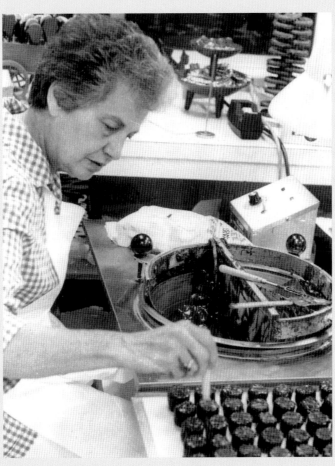

Pennsylvania, and from them produced and sold chocolate directly to area consumers. In 1930, the Philadelphia operation was relocated to Lititz. Shortly thereafter, the Newark plant was sold back to Albert Brewster, and Wilbur-Suchard excelled not only in retail but the wholesale market as well. Among the most desired items of the time were Suchard's chocolate squares and pastel purple-wrapped chocolate bars. Of course, the Wilbur Bud continued to bloom.

Even so, in 1958, Wilbur stopped the making and selling of Suchard products as their relationship ended. MacAndrews and Forbes Company bought the Wilbur Chocolate Company and it became a wholly owned subsidiary; in 1980, the company changed hands four more times, finally resting under the ownership of Cargill, Inc., in 1992. One of the largest private companies in the United States, Cargill deals mainly in the grain trade and agricultural commodities. Lest we think Wilbur Chocolate is just a minnow in this merger Jacuzzi, it acquired a chocolate facility in Mt. Joy, Pennsylvania, from the Bachman Candy Company, and in 2002, it bought the Canadian company Omnisweet, renaming it Wilbur, Limited. Later that year, Wilbur also purchased Peter's Chocolates from Nestlé, a leading supplier of premium chocolates, to further the campaign to boost its repertoire.

Located on the ground floor of the Lititz facility, the Wilbur Candy Americana Factory Store sells millions of Wilbur Buds — and much more. Customers can hear the sounds and smell the smells of the factory operating above while perusing the goods in an old-time candy-store setting. The experience includes demonstrations of candy-making in a viewing kitchen, as the staff makes fudge by hand and dips fresh chocolates on the premises.

While at the classic factory, one must visit the Candy Americana Museum, started in 1972 by Penny Buzzard, wife of former Wilbur president John Buzzard. Her hobby, now on display, was to scour flea markets, auctions, antique shows, and perhaps dark alleys in search of chocolate memorabilia like wrappers, molds, tins, and boxes. In time, vintage candy-making equipment like cooking kettles and marble slabs found its way to the museum from business associates and private stashes. The museum also features a collection of hand-painted, antique porcelain chocolate pots, along with huge display cases of ephemera and advertising.

Although Wilbur Chocolate Company had more business hook-ups than most, it retains a strong identity in the chocolate industry, delivering its tasty traditions through Wilbur Buds, the classic Wilbur factory store, and Mrs. Buzzard's memorable candy museum.

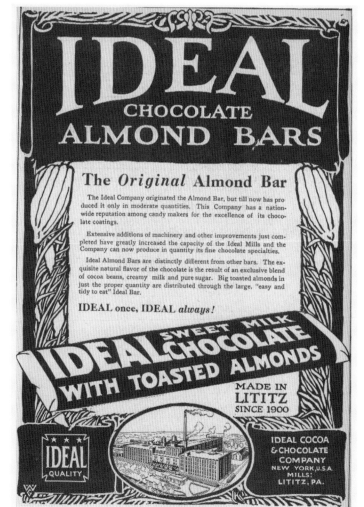

(Right) Wilbur Buds, dollops of chocolate molded with a flower bud imprint, remain sweet sellers for Wilbur Chocolate Company.
Courtesy Wilbur Chocolate Museum/Cargill

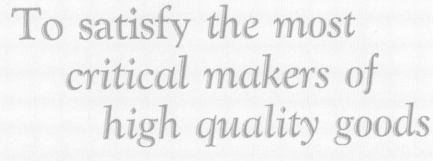

World's Finest Chocolate Company

Capone. Lucky Luciano. Hefner. Opler, Sr. Chicago in the first half of the twentieth century was home to a string of men who built their livelihoods, their reputations, and their empires on the tastes and temptations of the public. In doing so, these entrepreneurs of pleasure demolished the notion that the sinfully delicious, lascivious delights in life could only be had by the few, the moneyed, the upper crust. No matter what had to be done to succeed in their respective fields, these shrewd businessmen dirtied their hands to accomplish the dream of giving the common man his heart's most luxurious desires.

Ed Opler, Sr. moved to Chicago at age 18, hoping to tap into an underdeveloped cocoa market. His father died when he was 13 years old, and he quit school to support his family. For five years, he sold cocoa to bakeries around New York City via horse and buggy, developing a keen knowledge of the industry. In 1935, the young Depression-era entrepreneur laid the foundation of what was to be Chicago's own World's Finest Chocolate Company. Opler purchased a modest half interest in ingredient supplier Siren Mills, which produced tons of chocolate and cocoa for bakeries and dairies in Illinois cow country. He soon saw a sweet prospect.

Four years later, Opler sold his piece of Siren Mills and started Cook Chocolate Company, Chicago. The name World's Finest first came into play in 1950 as a sales division of Cook. Although trademarked in 1956, the now ubiquitous World's Finest became the company's official corporate name in 1972.

In the interim, the company expanded into Canada by establishing a manufacturing and sales outfit, and Opler developed what was perhaps World's Finest's greatest chocolate-related innovation — fundraising through the sale of its products. Beginning in 1949 with World's Finest milk chocolate and almond bars, the institution has helped raise more than $3 billion for youth organizations with its chocolate products. Six billion chocolate candy bars have been sold to private schools, dance clubs, sports teams, and cheerleading squads across the United States. Together with a tradition of family ownership, commitment to quality, consistency, and taste, this altruistic move has in no small part given World's Finest its longevity.

While Opler, Sr. carved out a serious niche in the fund-raising category, others followed and adapted his sales strategy; wrapping paper, books, and boxed cards all became fund-raising tools. What makes World's Finest popular among those other choices is, of course, the chocolate advantage. For many children, selling World's Finest chocolate is their first taste of being an independent entrepreneur. Today, between 90 and 95 percent of the company's revenues come from fundraising.

Although World's Finest follows the same recipe that was used more than fifty years ago in concocting its chocolate, the company keeps pace with the newest technology. One of only ten U.S. companies that makes chocolate straight from the bean, the company established its own experimental cacao plantation on St. Lucia, West Indies, in 1975. To formulate its special recipe, three different types of beans are blended. Cacao beans are then transformed to iconic World's Finest chocolate bars at the plant, located in an former Montgomery Ward distribution center on Chicago's Southwest Side.

Prior to 2003, World's Finest products were only available as marketing tools that could be customized according to the client's needs — fundraising candy, promotional, and corporate gifts. But before long, the company introduced its first branded retail product line. It used to require finding a Boy Scout or being a part of a Little League to get World's Finest Chocolate. Now, individuals can buy the tasty goods, from Caramel Whirls to seasonal gifts, at retail stores. World's Finest chocolate bar has been a rite of passage for anyone involved in youth-oriented fundraising in the past fifty years, but the famous candy bar is merely the beginning. The company now makes panned candy and even produces a version of a Mint Meltaway. Next time the doorbell rings and the recognizable white corrugated box shows up, peel a bill from your wallet for a classic chocolate treat.

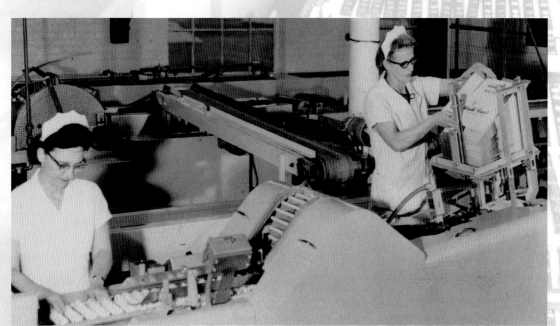

The World's Finest fundraising business began when a school band from Zion High School, outside of Chicago, asked Ed Opler Sr. if they could have chocolate bars to sell on consignment and raise money for new instruments.
Courtesy World's Finest Chocolate Company

145

INTRODUCTION TO CHOCOLATE MAKING:

How to Taste and Make Chocolate

CHAPTER SEVEN

Working with Chocolate

Chocolate is extremely fun to work with, and the results are often well worth the efforts. For best results, always use good quality ingredients, read recipes thoroughly, and use clean, dry utensils. There are a few other guidelines that are necessary to note in order to make delicious chocolate items.

STORAGE

It is best to store chocolate in a cool, dry place, as chocolate is sensitive to both heat and light. Also, make sure other odors don't migrate into the chocolate; keep it well-wrapped or in an airtight container. Dark chocolate generally lasts longer than milk chocolate.

MELTING CHOCOLATE

Do not burn or scorch chocolate. Once the cocoa butter has burned, chocolate is not useable. Always heat chocolate using low temperatures.

When melting chocolate, use a double boiler or the water-bath method, using a heatproof bowl that sits snugly over a saucepan. With either method, exercise caution when moving the top compartment from water. Water causes chocolate to seize, or turn stiff and gritty as the cocoa butter and solids separate, making it vital that all water — condensation, wet pans, and wet utensils included is kept out of the melting process. Always stir chocolate with a clean, dry rubber spatula to ensure even heating.

If seizing does occur, try to correct it by adding a small amount of vegetable oil and stirring the mix. This may bind the chocolate and make it smooth and workable again.

For melting purposes, a microwave can work too, but be sure to test the method on low power.

TEMPERING

This is the process of heating and cooling chocolate in order to stabilize the cocoa butter. Tempered chocolate, when cooled and hardened, is shiny and has a proper snap. Both conditions are necessary for molding, candy, and coating work.

To temper one pound of dark chocolate:

MELT. Cut the chocolate into half-inch pieces, and place two-thirds of it in a dry, clean bowl. Melt over a pan of simmering water. Stir from time to time until completely melted.

HEAT. Heat the chocolate to a temperature of 120 degrees Fahrenheit (115 degrees for white or milk chocolate). Use an accurate chocolate or candy thermometer.

COOL. Add the remaining one-third of the chocolate and stir with rubber spatula until it is completely melted. The temperature should be between 87 to 91 degrees (84 to 88 degrees for white or milk chocolate). If chocolate is too hot, let it sit for a few minutes until cool.

MAINTAIN TEMPERATURE. Use the tempered chocolate immediately, check the temperature frequently. Briefly re-warm the chocolate, as needed, over a pan of simmering water. Do not allow the temperature to rise above 91 degrees (88 degrees for white or milk chocolate), as the chocolate will go out

of temper. Overheated chocolate can be cooled down by "seeding" it with unmelted pieces. It must then be heated to proper temper again. Do not allow the temperature to fall below 85 degrees (this temperature is the same for dark, white, or milk chocolates), as solid bits may form.

DARK CHOCOLATE TEMPER RANGE:

Hold between 87° to 91° F

WHITE/MILK CHOCOLATE TEMPER RANGE:

Hold between 84° to 88° F

TASTING CHOCOLATE

Chocolate comes in many tastes, shapes, and forms. The best way to understand what is truly pleasing to you is to taste it regularly. Someone told me that the only way to understand chocolate is to learn its language. To comprehend chocolate, pay close attention to the product. Here's a mini-language lesson to get started.

To choose a fine chocolate for either baking or eating, start by looking on the package for the ingredients. Good quality chocolate should include cocoa liquor or cocoa mass, sugar, vanilla, cocoa

RIBBON CARAMELS.
(See Page 47.)

ALMOND FONDANT BALLS.
(See Page 52.)

DOUBLE FUDGE.
(See Page 43.)

ROSE AND PISTACHIO
CHOCOLATE CREAMS.
(See Page 53.)

WALNUT CREAM CHOCOLATES.
(See Page 52.)

ALMOND FONDANT STICKS.
(See Page 51.)

butter, and lecithin. Milk chocolate will list milk or cream. Anything else will get in the way of tasting real chocolate flavor, unless it is meant to be there, like a fruit or nut inclusion.

After unwrapping, look at the chocolate and notice the finish. Properly stored chocolate should have a nice gloss with no bloom or discolorations. Chocolates dark in color are usually those with more cocoa content, while typically lighter chocolates have milk content.

Next, chocolate quality can be discerned by a simple snap test. The chocolate should break with a nice clean snap and not crumble or bend. It should look consistent throughout. A fine chocolate has been conched for a lengthy period of time, and that should make the bar smooth looking.

Smelling chocolate can be truly revealing. Give your favorite bar a whiff and see if you can pick up hints about why you like it or what it contains. The finest chocolate smells like chocolate straight away. Sometimes hints of caramel or vanilla are easy to detect. It should not smell like the packaging it was wrapped in or, of course, sour or rancid.

The moment of truth is in the tasting. The technical term for what happens in the mouth is quite literally referred to as the "mouthfeel." Chocolate should feel smooth and velvety throughout, without grittiness. Chocolates made with real cocoa butter melt quickly and release additional hints and flavors. Taste is completely subjective, and the best way to find out what is good is to simply eat a lot on a regular basis.

A fun way to taste and compare is by buying chocolates within a category. Start with milk and white chocolate, working your way to dark chocolate with a green tea palate cleanser in between. It's also interesting to taste single-origin chocolates made from beans from one region compared with blended bean bars.

The wide world of chocolate is fascinating and fun. The best thing about it is that, while many chocolates are widely available, it seems there is always a new one to taste.

CHOCOLATE RECIPES

Table of Contents

Sag Harbor Double Chocolate Cheesecake

This is a dense, rich delight that was inspired by my new favorite cheese shop in Sag Harbor, Long Island. It is not too sweet and has a hint of mocha from the bit of coffee infused into the cheese. The turbinado sugar adds a slight molasses essence giving the sweet cheese flavor a unique profile. Make a Cocoa Pie Crust in advance and serve the next day for best texture and taste. This recipe makes enough filling for two pies.

Ingredients:

1/2 cup sour cream

2 tsps vanilla extract

2 tsps instant coffee

4 oz. unsweetened chocolate, finely chopped

4 oz. bittersweet chocolate, finely chopped

1 8-oz. pkg cream cheese, softened

15 oz. ricotta cheese

4 tbsps unsweetened cocoa

1/4 tsp salt

1 1/4 cups turbinado sugar

3 eggs, at room temperature

Cocoa Pie Crust (see recipe on page 159) or store-bought crust

Set oven temperature to 300 degrees Fahrenheit. Stir sour cream, vanilla, and instant coffee together in a small bowl. Set aside and mix occasionally until coffee completely dissolves. Melt both chocolates together in a double boiler over simmering water, stirring with a rubber spatula. Set aside and cool slightly. In a stand mixer fitted with the paddle attachment, beat cream cheese, ricotta cheese, cocoa, and salt until very smooth and fluffy. Scrape down the sides of the bowl and paddle frequently with each ingredient addition. Add sugar and continue beating until well blended. Scrape cooled chocolate into mixer bowl and beat until blended. Beat in sour cream mixture until well blended. Add eggs, one at a time, and beat until just blended. Do not overbeat. Pour filling into a pre-baked Cocoa Pie Crust, spread evenly, and smooth top. Bake 45 minutes or until set and middle is firm. The cheesecake will be slightly puffed, with a few cracks around the edge. Let cool to room temperature on a rack, then refrigerate until chilled (three hours or overnight) for the best texture and flavor.

Chocolate Buttermilk Olive Oil Cake

Beautiful moments sometimes happen from accidents, and this is one. I was out of vegetable oil, but I did have a deluxe bottle of olive oil my friend Ann Berger had given me for Christmas. Substitution out of desperation worked, and the result is a moist and astounding cake.

Ingredients:

1 2/3 cups flour

1 cup sugar

1/2 cup unsweetened cocoa

1 tsp baking soda

1/2 tsp salt

1 cup buttermilk (or sour milk)

1/2 cup extra virgin olive oil

2 tsps vanilla

Set oven to 350 degrees Fahrenheit. Butter and lightly flour 9 x 9-inch pan. Mix dry ingredients — flour, sugar, cocoa, baking soda, and salt — in a bowl. Add buttermilk, olive oil, and vanilla, beating until smooth. Spread in pan and bake 30 minutes. If completely cooked, a toothpick inserted in the center will come out clean. Cool 5 minutes in the pan before transferring to a wire rack.

Chocolate Cupcakes

These are simple and delicious little cakes. They can be dressed up with a fancy frosting flower or cursive frosting name for a special occasion. Makes about 18 cupcakes.

Ingredients:

2 cups all-purpose flour, sifted

1 tsp baking soda

1/4 tsp salt

1/2 cup unsweetened cocoa powder

3/4 cup sweet butter

1 tsp pure vanilla extract

1 1/2 cups sugar

3 large eggs

1 cup milk

Set oven to 350 degrees Fahrenheit. Prepare two cupcake tins with foil cup liners and set aside. Sift together dry ingredients — flour, baking soda, salt, and cocoa — in medium bowl and set aside. In a large bowl cream butter with an electric mixer. Add vanilla and sugar and mix. Add eggs one at a time, beating until smooth after each addition and scraping the bowl with a rubber spatula as necessary to keep the mixture smooth. Turn mixer to low speed, and alternately add dry ingredients in three additions with milk in two additions. Continue to scrape the bowl with spatula and beat only until smooth. Do not overbeat. Spoon batter into prepared tins, filling the cups only two-thirds. There is no need to smooth the tops; the batter will level itself in baking. Bake for 18 minutes or until tops spring back when lightly pressed with fingertips. Do not overbake. Cool cakes in pans 2 to 3 minutes. Remove and cool on a rack before icing with Bittersweet Chocolate Cupcake Icing (see recipe on page 157) or other favorite.

Bittersweet Chocolate Cupcake Icing

This icing is a silky chocolate glaze or dip for fresh baked cupcakes. I use bittersweet chocolate.

Ingredients:

6 oz. bittersweet chocolate

1/3 cup heavy cream

1 tbsp sugar

1 1/2 tbsps sweet butter

Place all ingredients in a small, heavy saucepan over low heat. Cook, stirring occasionally, until chocolate is partially melted. Remove from heat and stir constantly until chocolate is completely melted and mixture is smooth. Transfer to a small shallow bowl. Let stand about 10 minutes, stirring occasionally until icing reaches room temperature. Hold cupcake upside down and dip top into icing. Twirl cake slightly and continue to hold upside down for a few seconds to allow excess icing to drip off. Repeat with all of the cakes. Then, after dipping each once, double dip for a thick, even covering. When icing gets low, transfer to a smaller bowl or cup to maintain a smooth finish.

Fudge Tart

This recipe is adapted from one that appeared in an early Martha Stewart book. I have made it many times, and it is now a chocolate standard for me. Martha taught many of us how to make things we would not have dreamed of otherwise, and I thank her for the inspiration.

Ingredients:

5 oz. semisweet chocolate, finely chopped

3/4 cup (1 1/2 sticks) unsalted butter, cut into small pieces

1 1/2 cups turbinado sugar

2/3 cups all-purpose flour

6 eggs, lightly beaten

Cocoa Pie Crust
(see recipe on page 159)
or store bought-crust

Set oven temperature to 350 degrees Fahrenheit. Melt chocolate and butter together in a double boiler over simmering water. When completely melted, remove from heat and stir with rubber spatula to combine. Set aside to cool. Combine sugar, flour, and eggs in a mixing bowl and whisk until well blended. Stir in chocolate-butter mixture. Pour filling into a pre-baked pie crust and bake for approximately one hour and 15 minutes, until filling is set. Remove to a rack and let cool completely before serving. Tarts serve well with ice cream or a berry sauce.

Cocoa Pie Crust

This basic pie dough works out nicely for many chocolate-based pies, tarts, and filled cakes. It is flaky yet sturdy enough to hold dense fillings. This recipe makes two 9-inch cocoa crusts.

Ingredients:

2 1/4 cups all-purpose flour

1 tsp salt

1 tsp granulated sugar

1/4 cup unsweetened powdered cocoa

1 cup (2 sticks) cold unsalted butter, cut into small pieces

1/4 cup ice water

Put flour, salt, sugar, and cocoa in the bowl of a food processor. All ingredients should be cold. Add small pieces of cold butter and process for approximately 10 seconds or just until mixture resembles coarse meal. (If mixing by hand, combine dry ingredients in large mixing bowl and use a pastry blender or two table knives to cut in butter until mixture resembles coarse meal. Slowly add ice-cold water, small drops at a time, while using hands to knead and mix the dough. If crumbly, add a little more water until it holds together without being wet or sticky.)

Add ice water drop by drop through feed tube, with processor running, just until dough holds together without being wet or sticky. Do not process more than 30 seconds.

Test dough by squeezing a small amount together. If it is crumbly, add a bit more water. Place dough on plastic wrap and press into a flat circle for easy rolling. Wrap dough in plastic and chill for at least one hour. Lightly butter pie dishes or tart pans. On a board floured with cocoa powder, roll out pastry to a thickness of 1/8-inch. Place pastry in tart pan or pie plate and press lightly into bottom edges and along the sides. Trim excess pastry using sharp paring knife or by rolling a rolling pin across the top of the pan. Crimp or decorate edges of pastry, if desired. Chill pastry-lined pan until ready to use. Unbaked pastry shells can be refrigerated, covered in plastic, for up to one day. Freeze for longer storage and thaw before baking. To pre-bake pie crust, place pie weights or dried beans on the foil-covered shell and bake at 350 degrees Fahrenheit for 12 minutes.

Dark Chocolate Crème Brûlée

I have always loved a custard or crème brûlée. This version is easy to make and easy on the tongue too.

Ingredients:

2 cups whipping cream

2 cups half & half

8 oz. semisweet chocolate, finely chopped

8 large egg yolks

1/3 cups and 8 tbsps sugar

Set oven to 300 degrees Fahrenheit. Over medium heat, bring cream and half & half to boil in a large heavy saucepan. Reduce heat to low, add chocolate, and whisk until melted and smooth. Remove from heat. Whisk yolks and 1/3 cup sugar in large bowl to blend. Gradually whisk in hot chocolate mixture. Strain. Divide custard among eight 3/4-cup custard cups. Place cups in a large baking pan. Add enough hot water to pan to come halfway up sides of cups. Bake until custards are set, about 50 minutes. Remove from water; chill two hours. Cover and refrigerate overnight. Preheat broiler. Sprinkle each custard with 1 tablespoon sugar. Broil until sugar turns golden, watching closely to avoid burning (about three minutes). Refrigerate until custards are set, about two hours.

Earl Grey Infused Chocolate Pudding

This ganache-style pudding is simple to make. It works well with the Earl Grey tea, as the bergamot citrus flavors blend agreeably with the rich chocolate.

Ingredients:

4 1/2 oz. bittersweet chocolate, finely chopped

1 3/4 cups light cream

1 tbsp loose Earl Grey tea

2 tbsps Grande Marnier

Put chocolate into large, heatproof bowl. Set aside. Bring cream to a boil. Add tea to hot cream and let stand five minutes; strain. Pour tea infused cream, bit by bit, onto chocolate. Use whisk to stir well, making a smooth emulsion. Add Grande Marnier. Pour into small glasses, or ramekins, and chill at least two hours. Serve with fresh cream.

Chocolate Bread Pudding

This is a pleasing belly filler. It is satisfying and dense, and the texture of the bread surrounded by the pudding makes every bite a new experience.

Ingredients:

4 cups day-old baguette or Italian bread, cut roughly into 1/2-inch cubes

3 cups half & half

1/2 cup sugar

1/8 tsp salt

10 oz. bittersweet chocolate, chopped

6 large eggs

1 tsp pure vanilla

2 tbsps unsalted butter, cut into bits

fresh unsweetened whipped cream

Generously butter a 2 1/2-quart soufflé dish. Put bread in dish and set aside. In a 2-quart saucepan, combine half & half, sugar, and salt; set to medium heat; and stir constantly until sugar is dissolved and mixture is hot but not boiling. Remove from heat and add chocolate. Let stand two minutes. Whisk gently until smooth. Lightly beat eggs in large bowl and slowly add chocolate mixture, whisking until combined. Stir in vanilla. Pour mixture over bread and let soak at room temperature, pressing bread down occasionally, for about one hour. Put oven rack in middle position and preheat oven to 325 degrees Fahrenheit. Place cut butter on top of pudding and set soufflé dish into a larger pan with water bath — a larger dish with several inches of water on bottom. Bake in oven in hot water bath until edge is set but the center still trembles slightly, 45 minutes to one hour. Cool pudding in dish on a rack. Pudding will set as it cools. Serve warm with simple unsweetened cream or add a chocolate sauce.

Amy Guittard's L'Harmonie Raspberry Truffles

Gary Guittard's daughter Amy helped develop these tasty raspberry truffles in the test kitchen of Guittard — America's oldest family-owned chocolate company. The floral notes of raspberry perfectly enhance the acidity of the dark chocolate.

Ingredients:

7 oz. (1 1/3 cups) E. Guittard L'Harmonie 64% dark chocolate, chopped

1/4 cup heavy cream

1 tbsp seedless raspberry preserves

1/2 cup finely sifted unsweetened cocoa powder

Combine chocolate, cream, and preserves in a small saucepan over very low heat, stirring constantly until melted and smooth. Chill about 3 hours or until firm enough to handle. Alternatively, chill overnight and let stand at room temperature until soft enough to scoop. Form into one-inch balls using a scoop or two teaspoons. Roll between palms of hands to smooth out balls. Roll truffles in cocoa powder. Refrigerate in airtight container until ready to serve. Serve at room temperature.

Perfect Chocolate Drops

Little treasure cookies. Small, sweet, and chocolatey!

Ingredients:

4 oz. bittersweet chocolate, broken into pieces

2 tbsps unsalted butter

1/2 cup sugar

1 large egg

6 tbsps all-purpose flour

1/2 tsp baking powder

1/2 tsp salt

1/2 tsp pure vanilla extract

Preheat oven to 350 degrees Fahrenheit. Coat large baking sheet with light coat of nonstick oil spray. In a medium saucepan over very low heat, stir chocolate and butter with a rubber spatula until both are almost melted. Remove from heat and continue to stir until chocolate is completely melted. Blend in sugar. Working quickly to prevent curdling, whisk in egg. Stir in flour, salt, vanilla, and baking powder to make a firm dough. Drop rounded tablespoons of cookie dough, about 1 1/2 inches apart, onto prepared baking sheet. Bake until cookies are set and tops are slightly crackly, 8 to 10 minutes. Let cool on baking sheet for about 2 minutes and transfer to a wire rack. Serve slightly warm or at room temperature. Cookies can be stored in a tightly covered container at room temperature for up to five days or frozen for a month.

Chocolate-covered Creams

These types of creams, also known as fondants, were classics when I worked for Fannie May Candies. This recipe is simple and will remind you of boxed chocolates from a bygone era.

Ingredients:

2 1/2 cups sugar

1 cup light cream

1 tbsp light corn syrup

1/4 tsp salt

3 tbsps unsalted butter

1 tbsp vanilla extract

24 oz. semisweet chocolate, chopped, or 24 oz. chocolate chips

butter or margarine

Generously butter a 9 x 13-inch baking pan. Butter a large cookie sheet and line with wax paper; set both aside. Prepare fondant by combining sugar, cream, corn syrup, salt, and butter in a heavy, tall-sided saucepan. Be sure to use a tall saucepan as the mixture will boil high in the pot.

Place pan over low heat and stir mixture with a wooden spoon until sugar dissolves completely and syrup comes to a boil. Avoid boiling over. Clip a candy thermometer to inside of pan and cook syrup, without stirring, until it reaches 240 degrees Fahrenheit. Immediately pour hot syrup into prepared baking pan. Let syrup cool undisturbed until bottom of pan feels slightly warm, about 10 minutes. Add vanilla and use heavy wooden spoon to stir lukewarm mixture until it forms a ball. Transfer fondant to a 1-gallon Ziploc bag, removing as much air from the bag as possible. Let fondant rest several minutes before continuing. With fondant sealed in bag, roll ball with the heel of your hand, lightly kneading until the fondant looks smooth and creamy, about 10 to 12 minutes. Open bag and roll pieces of fondant into balls. Place on prepared cookie sheet; set aside.

Dipping the fondant:

Melt 12 ounces semisweet chocolate in top of a double boiler set over hot water. If you don't have a double boiler, chocolate can melt in a heatproof bowl over a pot of hot

Cocoa Shortbread

water. Stir chocolate with clean rubber spatula and remove from heat when chocolate has melted completely. Add remaining 12 ounces chocolate to melted part and stir until completely melted and smooth. Check with candy thermometer; temperature should be between 88 to 90 degrees Fahrenheit. If chocolate is too cold, place it back over hot water until the temperature is in correct range. If chocolate is too hot, let it cool until desired temperature it reached. Chocolate is tempered when it dries evenly and glossy on the tip of an inserted knife. Fondant balls can be dipped into melted chocolate with a toothpick or fork. Be sure to remove excess chocolate by tapping on the side of the bowl. Place covered candy on wax paper, stirring chocolate occasionally between dips. Let sit uncovered at room temperature overnight. Store in an airtight container at room temperature for up to two weeks.

These are fun little cookies — not too sweet. Serve with hot cocoa and fresh whipped cream.

Ingredients:

1 cup (2 sticks) unsalted butter, softened

2/3 cup confectioners sugar

2 tsps vanilla extract

2 cups all-purpose flour

1/4 cup ground cocoa powder

1/2 tsp salt

Using an electric mixer, beat butter and sugar until creamy and smooth, about 2 minutes. Add vanilla and beat well. Mix in flour, cocoa, and salt on low speed until just combined. Form dough into a disk, wrap in plastic, and chill for at least 2 hours. Preheat oven to 300 degrees Fahrenheit. Roll dough between two wax paper sheets to 1/4-inch-thick rectangle. Use sharp knife to cut shortbread into 2-inch squares; place squares one inch apart on baking sheets. Prick tops with fork and bake for 15 to 18 minutes. Cool completely on wire rack.

Lowney's Classic Cocoa Brownies

This early brownie recipe comes from the *Lowney's Illustrated Cookbook* published in 1908. Lowney's was a popular chocolate maker and manufacturer.

Ingredients:

2 oz. unsweetened chocolate, coarsely chopped

1/2 cup unsalted butter, slightly softened

1 cup sugar

1/2 cup all-purpose flour

1/4 tsp salt

2 large eggs

1/2 cup walnuts or pecans, chopped

Preheat the oven to 350 degrees Fahrenheit. Grease an 8-inch square baking pan or coat with nonstick spray. In a small heavy saucepan, melt chocolate over lowest heat, stirring frequently until it is nearly melted. Immediately remove from heat, stirring until completely melted. Let cool slightly. Using a large wooden spoon and working in a medium-sized bowl, beat together butter and sugar until well blended and smooth. Stir in chocolate until smoothly incorporated. Stir in all the remaining ingredients until well blended. Turn out batter into baking pan, smoothing to edges. Bake on center rack for 20 minutes, until a toothpick inserted in the center comes out clean. Cool on wire rack until thoroughly cooled. Use large sharp knife to cut brownies into squares, wiping knife clean between cuts. The brownies will keep in an airtight container for several days.

Fannie Farmer's Chocolate Meringue Cookies

Fannie Farmer was a cooking pioneer. A slight variation of her name went on to grace a chain of classic American candy stores — Fanny Farmer stores — that are no longer in business. Her chocolate meringues are fluffy and desirable little discs.

Ingredients:

2 egg whites

8 tbsps sugar, preferably superfine

1 tsp vanilla extract

4 tbsps unsweetened cocoa

Preheat oven to 250 degrees Fahrenheit. Beat egg whites until stiff but not dry, and add 6 tablespoons sugar, a spoonful at a time, beating well between each addition. Add unsweetened cocoa to mixture. Add vanilla and fold in remaining sugar. Shape meringues on a cookie sheet with a pastry bag or spoon. Bake for 1 hour. Turn off oven and let meringues sit until cool and crisp.

Chocolate Slushy

Montezuma sometimes took his cocoa drink cold and frothy. He allegedly had his drink mixers climb surrounding mountains to retrieve ice in order to insure that his cocoa beverage was just the right cool temperature.

Today, all it takes is a few ingredients obtainable from a local store to make this frothy chocolate special. For an extra festive slush, try a batch adding four tablespoons of vanilla vodka. Don't forget to raise your goblet to Montezuma.

Ingredients:

4 oz. bittersweet chocolate, chopped

2 tsps unsweetened cocoa powder

2 tbsps sugar

1 1/2 cups milk

4 cups ice

whipped cream

vanilla vodka (optional)

Place chocolate in the top of a double boiler over simmering water, stirring occasionally until melted. Add cocoa powder and sugar, stirring with a rubber spatula until thoroughly blended. Remove from heat and slowly add 1/2 cup milk and stir until smooth. Let mixture stand about 10 minutes until it reaches room temperature. Place remaining milk in a blender with cooled chocolate mixture and ice. Blend on high speed until smooth yet still frothy. Do not overblend. Pour into an oversized, festive drink glass, top with fresh whipped cream, and sprinkle with cocoa powder.

Beverages

The Vermeer Vanillion

Chocolate and vanilla are best buddies, and this drink that honors our two favorite pods is here to prove it. This makes a great dessert treat or nightcap.

Ingredients:

1/2 cup Vermeer Dutch Chocolate
　　Cream Liqueur

1/3 cup vanilla vodka

2 tbsps sugar

ice

Place ice and liquid beverage ingredients in drink shaker and shake well. Pour into glass with a sugar-coated rim.

Acknowledgements

This book is possible because of support from friends and family, industry experts, and everyday chocolate fans too. Thank you for your chocolate samples, suggestions, recipes, and rules.

A deep thanks goes out to the New York Public Library and the Frederick Lewis Allen Memorial Room. Each provided a precious haven from New York City bustle and a glorious place to study about chocolate.

Chris Bauch is an amazing agent/advisor. She gave time and support to this project and continues to be a sensible guide for future endeavors.

Michael Rosenberg is the president of Promotion In Motion and the owner of one extraordinary candy collection. The American Museum of Candy History will be made possible by his vision and carefully assembled objects.

Louise Brown from the Wilbur Chocolate Museum was kind enough to share Penny's collection, Wilbur Buds, and an outstanding chocolate memorabilia guide with me.

Curtis Vreeland and Eric Case inspired me with fine food at Maricel Presilla's restaurant. Maricel is a superior chef, accurate historian, and author extraordinaire. The oven at her Hoboken, New Jersey, restaurant, Cucharamama, is a superb source of excellent meals.

Myrna Fossum was a splendid hostess and instructive chocolate taste consultant. She remains a select friend and mentor.

Kate Berger was an awesome, all-around help. She is an effective and smart young human.

Matt Roland helped with research and left me with good details and abundant laughter.

Craig Kanarick helped with the cover concept. May he continue with his candy-inspired photo journey.

Dennis Durban from Nestlé went the extra mile by playing historian.

Will Noonan was once again an able and willing chocolate taster. He is the best friend and partner a candy girl could have.

Jim Gay, epicure from Historical Foodways in Colonial Williamsburg, granted me informative details about early American chocolate. I have a feeling there is a great work on chocolate lurking in his mind.

Ray, Peg, and Peggy Broekel sent back-up copies of Candy Bar Gazebo, still a valuable resource for those of us determined to understand the anthropology of candy.

Warren and Jill Schimpff are encouraging, kindred spirits who share a passion for vintage items and good confections. Started in 1891, G.A. Schimpff's Confectionery is one of the oldest, family-owned candy businesses in the United States.

Marlene Machut set up discussions with John Lunde and Harold Schmitz at Mars, Inc., that were fascinating and could have lasted for days.

Susan Smith with the Chocolate Manufacturers Association was helpful with support, stats, and industry information.

Clay Gordon gave me time, resources, and material that made my discovery processes extra interesting. Thanks for being the chocophile that you are.

Andes Mints are featured on the cover because Owen Nelson took the time to tell me a little about his story. His father-in-law, Andrew Kanelos, founded Andes Candies.

Lake Champlain Chocolate shared its factory, chocolate, and history with me. Lake Champlain is truly a five-star American chocolatier.

E. Guittard Vintage Chocolates supplied blocks for photos and experimenting. I used this chocolate in testing my recipes and was so pleased with the results. I am a better chocolatier thanks to Guittard.

Madelaine Chocolates hosted me for a tour day; shared their fascinating story; and were, as always, gracious, genuine, and fun.

The following companies courteously supplied chocolate products for the cover image, recipe testing, and inspiration: Guittard, Christopher Norman, Godiva, Scharffen Berger, Madelaine, Van Duyn, and Moonstruck.

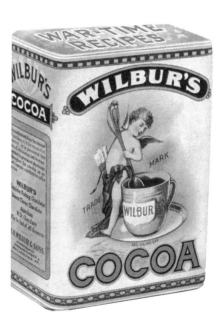

Chocolate Bibliography

American Craft Museum. *Confectioner's Art.* New York: American Craft Council, 1988.

Broekel, Ray. *The Great American Candy Bar Book.* Boston: Houghton Mifflin Company, 1982.

Coady, Chantal. *The Chocolate Companion: A Connoisseur's Guide to the World's Finest Chocolates.* New York: Quintet Publishing Limited, 1995.

Coe, Sophie D. and Michael D. Coe. *The True History of Chocolate.* London: Thames and Hudson Inc., 1996.

Cunningham, Marion and Lauren Jarrett. *The Fannie Farmer Cookbook.* New York: Knopf, Anniversary Edition, 1996.

Daley, Regan. *In the Sweet Kitchen: The Definitive Baker's Companion.* New York: Artisan, 2001.

Fernandez-Armesto, Felipe. *Near a Thousand Tables: A History of Food.* New York: Free Press, 2002.

González, Elaine. *The Art of Chocolate: Techniques & Recipes for Simply Spectacular Desserts & Confections.* San Francisco: Chronicle Books, 1998.

Heatter, Maida and Toni Evins. *Maida Heatter's Book of Great Chocolate Desserts.* New York: Random House, 1995.

Hershey Foods Corporation Staff. *Hershey's 1934 Cookbook.* New York: Smithmark Pub, Revised & Expanded edition, 1999.

Jacobsen, Rowan. *Chocolate Unwrapped: The Surprising Health Benefits of America's Favorite Passion.* Montpelier: Invisible Cities Press, 2003.

Jayne-Stanes, Sara. *Chocolate: The Definitive Guide.* London: Grub Street, 1999.

Lopez, Ruth. Chocolate: *The Nature Of Indulgence*. New York: Harry Abrams, Inc., 2002.

Marcus, Adrianne. *The Chocolate Bible*. New York: G. P. Putnam Sons, 1979.

Medrich, Alice and Deborah Jones.*Bittersweet: Recipes and Tales from a Life in Chocolate*. New York: Artisan, 2003.

Morton, Marcia and Frederic. *Chocolate: An Illustrated History*. New York: Crown Publishers, 1986.

Presilla, Maricel E. *The New Taste of Chocolate: A Cultural & Natural History of Cacao with Recipes*. Berkeley: Ten Speed Press, 2001.

Richardson, Tim. *Sweets*. New York: Bloomsbury, 2002.

Stewart, Martha. *Martha Stewart's Pies and Tarts*. New York: Clarkson Potter, 1992.

Tannahill, Reay. *Food in History*. New York: Three Rivers Press, Revised edition, 1995.

Resource for Delicious American Chocolates

Bissinger's

McPherson Store
4742 McPherson Avenue
Saint Louis, Missouri 63108
314.367.9750
bissingers.com

B. T. McElrath Chocolatier

2010 East Hennepin Avenue
Minneapolis, Minnesota 55413
612.331.8800
btmcelrath.com

Dagoba Organic Chocolate

POB 5330
Central Point, Oregon 97502
541.664.9030
dagobachocolate.com

Ghyslain Chocolatier

350 West Deerfield Road
Union City, Indiana 47390
765.964.7905
ghyslain.com

Guittard Chocolate Company

10 Guittard Road
Burlingame, California 94010
650.697.4427
guittard.com

Knipschildt Chocolatier

4 New Canaan Avenue
Norwalk, Connecticut 06851
203.849.3141
knipschildt.com

Lake Champlain Chocolates

750 Pine Street
Burlington, Vermont 05401
802.864.1807
lakechamplainchocolates.com

Scharffen Berger Chocolate Maker

914 Heinz Avenue
Berkeley, California 94710
800.930.4528
scharffenberger.com

Vosges Haut-Chocolat Boutiques

132 Spring Street
New York, New York 10012
212.625.2929
vosgeschocolate.com

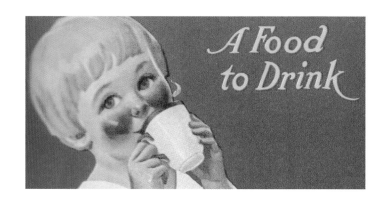